The Slavery Tax Rate

Allopoly Theory

by

Alain Hadges

MEI Publications, LLC

MEI Publications LLC

The Slavery Tax Rate: Allopoly Theory
1st Edition. May 2021

ISBN: 978-0-9964681-2-1

www.slaverytaxrate.com

In memory of:

Maria Eugenia Ibrán

George Nicholas

Acknowledgments

Special thanks to:

Joe Borini

Paul Shearman Allen

Table of Contents

Index of Tables..9
Table of Figures..10
Foreword..11
Context..13
Theory...17
   Abstraction...21
   Structure..21
   Government..23
   Imputed Morality...24
   Benefits..25
   The Accumulation of Imposed Allopolistic Loss.................25
   Comparative Advantage..26
   Cooperation, Secrecy, Coercion and Force.........................26
   Dishonesty...27
   Collusion..27
   Simultaneous Operation of Multiple Effects......................28
   Communication...28
   Travel...30
   Anonymity..31
   Education..31
   Quality of Life...32
   Diffuse Acquisition and Concentrated Collection...............33
   Allopoly Prevention..35
   Allopoly Progression...36
   Allopoly Succession..37
   Standards..39
   Values...41
   Cascading Allopolistic Loss due to Dishonesty..................42
   Rule and Law Violations and Changes................................42
   Technology..45
   Foreseeable End..47
   Allopoly versus Culture...49
   Law..51
   The Cycle of Civilization..52
   Measurement..55
   Time as an Economic Measure...57
   Time, Culture, Education and Technology...........................60
   Analytical Implications..66
   Non-Government Allopolies...67
   Government Allopolies..67
   Corruption..68

Oversight...70
  Draining the Swamp..71
The Cycle of Civilization (with Time as a Metric).......................77
  The Rise of a Civilization..77
  The Decline of a Civilization.....................................78
Time vs. Currency..79
Population Density, Mobility and Resources..............................80
Allopolistic Characteristics of Slavery..81
The Slavery Tax Rate...83
  Slavery Scenario 1..84
  Slavery Scenario 2..85
The Slavery Tax Rate of Government Workers (STR$_W$)................86
Interpretation of the Slavery Tax Rate for Government Workers. 90
Government Workers...92
  Federal Government Workers...................................93
  State Government Workers.......................................93
  County Government Workers.....................................93
  Municipal Government Workers...............................93
Population..94
Computation of the Slavery Tax Rate of Government Worker Costs
....94
Number of United States Government Hierarchies......................96
The Slavery Tax Rate for Non-Labor Costs (STR$_N$) and Specific
Amounts...96
  Calculation of the Slavery Tax Rate for Government Non-Labor
  Costs and Specific Amounts.....................................96
  Inherent Fairness of the Slavery Tax Rate Calculation............99
  Summing the Slavery Tax Rate for Labor, Non-Labor
  Government, and specific Costs................................100
Government Interest Payments..101
Government Transfer Payments...102
Regressive Taxes..103
Business Taxes...104
Implementation..104
The Slavery Tax Rate Using Real Data.......................................105
Questions...110
  Spouses and Significant Others...............................113
  Children...113
  Retirees..113
  Unemployment..114
  The Elderly...116
  Specific Interpretation of the Slavery Tax Rate.......118
  The Infirm...120

The Indigent..120
Pensions..121
Medicine..121
The Incarcerated and Other Government Wards....................121
Resources with Inelastic Demand...................................127
Summary..133
Data Consistency Checks..134
Federal Government Employment Data.............................134
U.S. Bureau of Labor Statistics Current Employment Survey
Data Exclusions (CE Series)..135
U.S. Office of Personnel Management Data Exclusions.........135
State Government Employment Data................................136
U.S. Bureau of Labor Statistics Current Employment Survey
Data Exclusions (SM Series)...137
Individual State Comprehensive Annual Financial Report State
Government Employee Exclusions....................................137
References..138
Appendix A: 2018 U.S. Population, Income, Federal Government
Workers and Unemployment...145
Appendix B: 2018 State Population, Income, State + Local
Government Workers and Unemployment...........................145
Appendix C: U.S. Office of Personnel Management Federal
Employment Data Reference And Comparison.....................147
Appendix D: Comparison of State Government Employment Data
Between U.S. Bureau of Labor Statistics SM series and
Individual State 2019 Comprehensive Annual Financial Reports
....148
Appendix E: Individual State Comprehensive Annual Financial
Report (CAFR) Source Data Reference...............................151
Appendix F: Arithmetic Refresher....................................152
Alphabetical Index...153
Index of Theorems...156
Index of Corollaries..157
Index of Questions...158
What is next?...159

Index of Tables

Table 1: Slavery Tax Rate shown as Population to Government Worker ratio..89

Table 2: Illustration of the slavery tax rate (c_P) computation for non-labor costs (C_P) of $1,000, for a population of ten people, with a standard work year (S_Y) of 2,000 hours.................98

Table 3: Slavery Tax Rate Data for Washington D.C., 2018.........106

Table 4: Slavery Tax Rate Data for Wyoming (WY), 2018.............107

Table 5: Comparison of Total Federal Employee Count published data: U.S. Bureau of Labor Statistics CE series data versus U.S. Office of Personnel Management Federal Workforce data and U.S. Department of Defense...........................134

Table 6: Comparison of State Employee Count published data: U.S. Bureau of Labor Statistics SM Series data* vs State Comprehensive Annual Reports for All States and the District of Columbia...136

Table of Figures

Figure 1:   United States Average and Median Net Wages...............32

Figure 2:   Slavery Tax Rate (STR$_W$) as Percent of the Individual's Time vs Total Imposed Tax vs P/G Ratio.........................90

Figure 3:   2018 U.S. Slavery Tax Rate by State using the working age population 18 to 64 years. (excluding non-labor costs). 108

Figure 4:   2018 U.S. Slavery Tax Rate by State for the working age population ages 18-64 and a fixed unemployment amount*. (excluding non-labor costs)............................117

Figure 5:   2018 U.S. Slavery Tax Rate by State for the working age population ages 18-64, fixed unemployment amount* and retired ages 65+ with benefits at half the rate of standard work time. (excluding non-labor costs).........................119

Figure 6:   2018 U.S. Government Workers (Federal+State+Local) vs Total Population. Federal government workers apportioned using a G_F / $P_{[all]}$ ratio of 0.01674................123

FOREWORD

It is often said that private enterprise operates more efficiently than government. However, private enterprise has the tremendous advantage of a single metric to demonstrate precisely how well a business has been operated in the past and how well it is currently being run. This versatile metric also sets targets for future performance for any kind of private enterprise. It considers all operational efficiencies and inefficiencies, competence and incompetence and all decisions both helpful and detrimental. That metric is ***profit***.

Government operates differently from private enterprise. It currently has no single metric that can be used to measure how well it is run or set targets for future performance. Government does not offer goods or services based upon supply and demand. Instead, it imposes taxes and other costs on its population and uses force to take the taxes if the population refuses to pay.

This text proposes a single metric that is to government what the measurement of profit is to business. That metric is the ***slavery tax rate***, an objective measure of government performance with respect to the population and a visible target for government expenditures.

The term "slavery tax rate" raises an important question:

What tax rate makes a person a slave?

This question is as easy to ask as it is difficult to answer in objective terms. The challenge is that, although subjective responses and opinions abound, objective answers require quantifiable measurements. Specifically:

• How does one measure slavery?

- How does one measure freedom?
- Are they based upon the same measures, or do they differ?
- What marks the transition from freedom to slavery?

Many difficulties faced by elected officials, government planners and citizens are made visible by computing the slavery tax rate.

An understanding of what the slavery tax rate represents requires a shift in perspective in three areas:

- First, in the metrics typically used to define imposed costs, such as taxes, fines, etc. Imposed costs can take many forms. They may be visible, such as an income tax form, but they may also be invisible such as when they are part of the price of a good or service. Imposed costs can also take the form of opportunity costs, such as not having the time to obtain an education because of the need to work two jobs to support a family.
- Second, in the sources of imposed costs. Governments are not the only entities or organizations that impose costs on others.
- Third, in how an economy works. Because we must see the big picture, abstractions simplify the operation and continual changes of many complex social interactions.

Surprisingly, the pursuit of answers to these questions leads to a better understanding of why civilizations before ours have fallen. This connection is not as far-fetched as it may seem, as simple probability may attest. Consider the following:

We humans have forgotten much of our past. As we discover more of our history, the number of civilizations known to have crumbled has increased from single to double digits. Some historians believe that external causes such as conquest, the use of lead, drought or disease drive civilizations into decline or, at the very least, enable their overthrow, all seemingly after attaining the apex of technological advancement in their time. These and other externalities may well have contributed to the decline of some civilizations. However, accepting such externalities as the sole reason for the decline of entire civilizations also requires accepting that their occurrence is chance, the luck of the draw for that civilization. One must then wonder whether it is mere coincidence that such bad luck occurred to every civilization preceding our present one.

As it turns out, the same forces that drive the rise of civilizations also operate, in large part, to cause their ruin.

In this book, answers to these questions are developed and presented. Their logic and rationale are explained, and objective measures of the slavery tax rate are calculated using publicly available government data.

CONTEXT

The culture of any territory that can support a population can be envisioned to operate between two extremes. At one extreme is a vibrant economy where farmers, artisans and tradespeople live and enjoy their lives. At the other extreme are those same people, trudging under the watchful eyes of soldiers who flog them for not working hard enough, then throw them into cages for the night.

Historically, many feudal lords took what they wanted by force. Others were less heavy-handed and imposed a system of taxes. In more modern times, those in power who were sophisticated enough to control the currency of an economic system took what they wanted by creating cycles of inflation and deflation. The operational difference between them is that uneducated people understand the threat of force and can visualize what is being taken, such as money, goods or property. However, a substantial amount of education and information is required to understand how the same result is achieved through the manipulation of currency. Otherwise, this "taking" is invisible to most of the population, who simply see prices go up and down.

Throughout history, other rulers instilled an acquiescence to the taking such as removing their harvest or property, into their population from childhood, and even the belief that their lot in life was slavery. Still others turned their education system into an indoctrination system that used variants of operant conditioning.[1] The combinations and degrees of the means of taking from a population are infinitely variable, but the most efficient are those that result in the individual either willingly giving, not being aware of the taking, or at least not opposing it.

If one were, for example, to place a group of sufficiently skilled farmers, hunters, fishers and tradespeople in a wide, verdant valley, what would prevent a few from turning the rest into slaves?

Is it accurate to assume that a few individuals or groups of individuals would seek to turn the rest into slaves?

Perhaps, but we have not yet identified a driving force that would set those events into motion.

Would history necessarily repeat itself through the imposition of slavery?

Social dynamics are, in large part, based upon the knowledge and values of multiple individuals. Unlike experiments in the physical sciences, social experiments will not always yield repeatable results.

Governments clearly play a role in society. But what role, precisely? Traditional definitions of governments are not definitive so much as observations of the general operation of governments at points in time.

Because they are composed of many different people, governments are a shifting continuum of various types of activities and behaviors. Furthermore, the interactions between different parts of a government or even between individuals within different parts of a government and its citizens, can themselves be a defacto shifting continuum of government types. Furthermore, that is before subjectivity even enters the equation, let alone any motivation to slant subjective assessments.

E.g.: A totalitarian government espouses that its actions are for the good of its people while executing people trying to escape the boundaries of its regime.

Objectively categorizing a government requires a visible, objective measure. Ultimately a government is composed of people. The purpose and function of a government are to affect the lives of people.

Therefore, the distance from slavery or the degree of slavery that a government imposes upon its people could be such an objective metric.

But what is slavery?

Can you recall when you have heard the term **slavery** used, and the times you have used it? Most likely, each use of the term referred to a particular act or set of acts in particular circumstances.

A mindless response would be to say that slavery is tied to the current legal definition of slavery. Some cultures have laws that define slavery by ownership. Other cultures had a caste system that defined slavery, and yet other caste systems did not explicitly use the term **slavery** but had the same effect. Still other cultures used a combination of government and economic strata to achieve the same end. The implication was that slavery was recognized when it was overt but could not be defined in unequivocal, objective terms that could be used to identify it in all circumstances.

This is an astounding gap in our knowledge!

After all, slavery has been around since the beginning of humanity.

Why, then, is it difficult to define slavery in clearly measurable terms?

This analytical discontinuity has to do with the fundamental relationships of our own species, such as parent-child, employer-employee, guardian and agent, that are easy to define in unequivocal terms when analyzing social structures. Defining slavery in clear, objective terms is not easy. Therefore, one can conclude that the foundations of our analyses are flawed. In such a situation, we must develop the theory by which we define slavery from the ground-up.

The review of historical studies of slavery will be postponed until we better understand the nature of our inability to describe slavery in objective terms.

THEORY

We will start at the most basic level to determine the manifestation of slavery: the individual. We will then apply this approach to the government level. Let us start with a simple example that does not involve government.

EXAMPLE #1: The Robber

A couple is walking down a path. The couple has achieved their current quality of life by farming and taking their produce to market. A robber with a gun confronts them and takes all their valuables.

The robber's gun gives him a monopoly on coercion. However, the term **monopoly** is confusing in that its meaning is wrapped up in markets.[2] The existing vocabulary diverts the thought process away from the problem. We need a different word to avoid confusion with conventional definitions. That word should include all types of transactions over which control can be exerted, including not only transactions exercised by monopolies but also methods deemed illegal such as blackmail, extortion, coercion or even brainwashing. Let us call this word **allopoly**.

DEFINITION #1: Allopoly

The exclusive possession or control of people and resources through any means, whether legal or illegal, moral or immoral. The smallest allopoly is the individual.

Having defined this term, let us now test it. An allopoly applies to a commercial situation in which there is only one supplier of a good or service. It applies to the robber in the example. It also pertains to the magistrate who gives a favorable judgment at the request of the politician who appointed them. It applies in the case of an organization that prohibits nepotism, in which the managers of two different departments agree to hire each other's family members. It applies to the government of a country as well as its population. It applies to any group of people with control over other people, other allopolies and resources. It also applies to any individual creature in nature because, absent any external influence, each has control over themselves and is, therefore, an allopoly. In the negative, the fear of a state's allopolistic control of the federal government is why Washington D.C. was not created as a semi-sovereign state.[3]

As in conventional monopolies, by virtue of exclusive control, allopolies tend to yield greater returns for resources expended in an endeavor compared to operations that take place in a more competitive environment.

Unlike traditional economic analyses, allopoly theory assumes that all forms of control can be in play, be they legal, illegal, moral or immoral. To a system outsider, allopolies and thereby allopolistic activities may be difficult to perceive or measure due to the inherent lack of available information on prohibited or illegal actions. Measurement difficulties aside, the same economic principles of monopolies broadly apply to allopolies.

In our example, the robber with a gun pointed at his victim is an allopolist; his allopoly is coercive force. The robber will receive allopolistic profit from the endeavor, the illegal analog of monopolistic profit.

The couple in the example has a certain quality of life. Part of it is measured by their possessions, that is, their accumulated wealth. The robber's motive is to improve his own quality of life by reducing that of the couple he is robbing.

Is it greed that drives the robber so that the benefit is what is taken? Is it a basic need for subsistence that cannot be met in another way? Or is the value of the act to the robber some other type of gratification?

The term **greed** has many connotations, as do terms that relate to **desire**. Again, the vocabulary misdirects the thought process. Humans will generally want more of something they perceive to benefit them, until there is no perceived benefit to acquiring more. Instead of **greed**, another, more appropriate term may be used: **local non-satiation**.[4] It is a term devoid of unwanted or distracting connotations. With this, we now have our first working theorem.

THEOREM #1: The Driving Force of Allopoly Creation

The rational, locally non-satiable individual prefers to create allopolies because the returns on resources expended in allopolistic endeavors are generally greater than those gained in more competitive environments.

From one perspective, the example of the robber's forcible coercion of the couple was also an example of slavery, however fleeting, at the individual level. Yet, we still have no definition of **slavery**. Now let us try an example that shows a role of government.

EXAMPLE #2:   The Miners

A group of explorers and their families go into unexplored territory, dig a copper mine, extract the copper and trade their manufactured copper goods in city markets.

Bandits follow the miners back to their mine and extort the product of their labor by threat of force. For years, they force the miners to work excavating copper and making goods, which the bandits, in turn, take to market. The bandits take everything except the minimum subsistence to keep the miners alive and working. They even keep the miners in cages whenever they are not working.

At one point, another group of bandits attempts to take the mine away from the first group. But the first group of bandits fights them off, thus keeping the mine.

Eventually, the miners' sons grow up and overpower the bandits. The miners then pay some of their children to protect the mining community from bandits.

The miners had an allopoly on their mine. Their mining expertise is also an allopoly. Finally, they had an allopoly on their own time. The miners created an allopoly from these three allopolies to increase their quality of life. The new allopoly produced returns on the efforts expended upon it greater than would have been obtained in a competitive environment where everyone had a copper mine and knew how to extract, process and work copper.

The bandits formed their own allopoly of force and coercion, which they imposed upon the miners' allopoly, thereby creating a new combined allopoly. The bandits thus improved their quality of life by reducing that of the miners.

Abstraction

In the preceding example, the term *allopoly* was used for each low-level allopoly. It was also used for a higher-level allopoly created as a result of combining or merging the lower-level allopolies. When used in this manner, the term *allopoly* is an abstraction that simplifies the description of the operations of the constantly changing, growing, shrinking, newly created and disappearing social interactions, organizations and their structures that comprise allopolies.

The use of different descriptions for the types of allopolies, such as "sub-allopoly" and "sub-sub-allopoly", may seem appealing as a tracking mechanism but quickly becomes unwieldy.

Structure

In their allopoly over the miners, the return on the bandits' investment was greater than if the bandits had become employees of the miners and earned a wage for their labor. Either of the aforementioned allopoly structures, the bandits taking control of the mines by force or the bandits becoming paid labor for the miners, would have yielded allopoly profits from the mining operation. However, the benefit to any particular individual within an allopoly is a function of their position within it.

Allopolies are organizations of one or more entities, and these organizations may have an infinite number of forms between the two extreme distributions of control. At one end of the spectrum is the totalitarian form, where all control resides in a single individual. At the other end is the democratic form, where all organization members exercise the same level of control. Viewed another way, each allopoly has a total amount of control that it can exert internally and externally. The control of an allopoly is distributed among its members in many ways including partnerships, corporations, government, gangs, and any other form of delegation and oversight.

It follows from *THEOREM #1: The Driving Force of Allopoly Creation*, that a pyramid structure for organizational control will eventually form for the allopoly to function. Rare exceptions exist when the objectives, requisite actions and distribution of allopoly benefits are readily apparent to and enforceable by all allopoly members.

Without someone or some allopoly in control, in whatever form, the miners could not have coordinated their efforts and established their allopoly over copper goods. By the same token, without someone or some allopoly in control, the bandits could not have maintained their allopoly over the miners.

To lead within an allopoly, the top of the allopoly must have more control than the bottom. Greater control implies a smaller number of people, with each higher level being a smaller allopoly of increasing control. Each level has more control than the level beneath it. We have arrived at another theorem.

THEOREM #2:   Allopoly Structure

Allopolies will eventually form pyramid structures of control to maintain control over other allopolies and resources, with the greatest control residing at the top and the least control residing at the bottom.

Government

When the miners' children grew up, they overcame the bandits' allopoly on coercive force. This action mostly restored the miners' quality of life to what it had been before the bandits arrived. But, as we shall see, not entirely.

The miners thereafter needed to expend resources to maintain a police force to protect them from bandits. The miners' quality of life is better without the bandits' overlordship. However their quality of life is reduced from what it was before the bandits appeared by the amount the miners must pay for a police force, which is now a government function. With this example, some functional requirements of a government become clear.

DEFINITION #2: Government, Society, Culture and Civilization

A government is an allopoly over resources and other allopolies, as are societies, cultures, civilizations, families, gangs, and business organizations.

The first group of bandits protected themselves, and thus the miners, from the second group of bandits. In economic terms, the only difference between the first group of bandits and the paid police force of their children is that the paid police force reduced the miners' quality of life by less than the extortive regime of the first group of bandits did. Would that remain the case forever?

That question has already been answered by *THEOREM #1: The Driving Force of Allopoly Creation*: No, it would not. Because governments generally have an allopoly on coercive force over their population, they can create the most profitable allopolies. Therefore, governments are the preferred allopoly creation target of rational individuals exhibiting local non-satiation.

The converse is also true. Because of local non-satiation, given any kind of gain and the opportunity to achieve it, individuals in government will, eventually, form their own allopolies with others inside and outside of government. We have arrived at another theorem.

THEOREM #3:   Preference to Form Allopolies with Governing Allopolies

Rational locally non-satiable individuals will strive to form allopolies with, within, and of governing allopolies because of the latter's inherent power.

Imputed Morality

Implicit in *DEFINITION #1: Allopoly* and *THEOREM #1: The Driving Force of Allopoly Creation* is the absence of any kind of imputed morality on the part of government workers, at any level, be they elected officials, appointed officials, management, bureaucrats, judges, prosecutors, police officers, general staff or sanitation workers.

Morality is not part of the definition because a given population is composed of locally non-satiable individuals. Individuals in a culture will weigh the risks and rewards of their actions and act according to their risk tolerances. This includes all actions, be they legal, illegal, moral or immoral.

A government is an allopoly composed of individuals from the wider population. Therefore it is unreasonable to expect that the behavior of individuals in government will differ from the behavior of people in the general population.[5]

Benefits

Allopolies exist in every conceivable variety. Some will be easier than others to identify and measure. Certain allopolies will have little effect on those other than the allopolists themselves, such as an artist painting a self-portrait or a mathematician solving an equation. However, the benefits most allopolies provide for the allopolists come at the expense of other allopolies, such as pick-pockets working a shopping mall or a gang extorting protection money from a shopkeeper. The price exacted by one allopoly upon another need not be monetary. It may be any price that can be imposed, such as exerting control over another person or allopoly.

The result of the imposition of allopolistic loss is a degraded quality of life due to the imposed loss itself or the need to expend more resources or impose allopolistic loss on others to maintain the same quality of life. This outcome brings us to the next definition.

DEFINITION #3: Allopolistic Loss

Allopolistic loss is the gain by one allopoly that is imposed as a loss upon other allopolies. The loss can take many forms, which are not always money.

The Accumulation of Imposed Allopolistic Loss

The accumulation of allopolistic loss on all strata of a culture compounds and cascades. In simple terms, an increase in imposed allopolistic loss or taxes at an earlier level of a supply chain increases the prices and costs later in the supply chain. The imposition of allopolistic loss earlier in a supply chain is a means to disguise it as a price increase from those later in the supply chain.

Comparative Advantage

Allopolies of ability also exist. Thus, there are allopolies based upon comparative advantage.[6] However, the concept of comparative advantage is not as free of allopolistic loss as it might seem because a comparative disadvantage can be imposed.

E.g.: The deliberate exclusion from education of a segment of the population to be used for menial labor.

Cooperation, Secrecy, Coercion and Force

The mechanics of allopoly formation and maintenance are infinite in their variety. However, to survive, any particular allopoly must provide greater benefit to its members than could be extracted from it by other allopolies.

The ability of an allopoly to impose allopolistic loss upon others is a function of the disparity in the ability to apply force and coercion. Conversely, the ability of an allopoly to defend itself from the imposition of allopolistic loss is also a function of that disparity. Generally, the most efficient defense is to avoid targeting in the first place. Hence, secrecy is often the preferred method of allopoly defense. However, many allopolies cannot operate in secrecy and will attempt to defend themselves from the imposition of allopolistic loss.

COROLLARY #1: Allopoly Secrecy, Cooperation, Coercion, and Force

Allopolies are most easily formed and maintained where the allopolists can keep the allopoly secret (secrecy) and if not, can defend their allopoly from other allopolies and overcome resistance to the imposition of the allopolistic loss (cooperation, coercion and force). The choice between these is a function of the cost of each.

Dishonesty

Dishonesty is a tactic that can be used to obtain cooperation, conceal, coerce and apply force. The potential gains from dishonesty include convincing others, both inside and outside the allopoly, to do or not do what the allopolists want.

Dishonesty exists in myriad different types and variations, including an individual lying, document forgery, the planting or destruction of evidence, misleading, non-disclosure and propaganda. Depending on the circumstances, some approaches will be more effective than others. Dishonesty will likely occur in situations where the risk is low compared to the gain. Generally, the relatively low initial cost of dishonesty is a primary reason for its longevity, as even the earliest written laws tried to increase the risk of dishonesty.[7]

Collusion

Collusion is a form of cooperation that can greatly increase the chance that dishonesty and criminal acts will succeed, thereby reducing the associated risk for those involved. What makes collusion attractive is its low initial cost for the benefit it can bring.

At least one country, the United States, and a number of the semi-sovereign states of which it is composed have attempted to increase the risk for collusion among multiple actors by creating a separate crime called "conspiracy", with an additional penalty from the intended criminal act.[8]

E.g.: In a government department, certain managers fear that an employee will expose their improper activities. These managers conspire to falsely accuse the employee to discredit her and have the department dismiss the employee. The managers need not explicitly communicate their intent to collude, as each is aware of the consequences of not acting.

Simultaneous Operation of Multiple Effects

Up to this point we have covered three relatively simple theorems and one corollary. These theorems and corollaries can be seen as behavioral drivers. To do so, we must first accept that the degree of the resulting behavior will be a spectrum, not an absolute. Then, a fundamental reality comes into play: a few simple rules operating simultaneously may result in complex behavior.

Communication

One method an allopoly can use to avoid becoming a target is preventing the formation of other allopolies that would either attack it or reduce its ability to defend itself.

At the core of allopoly formation is some sort of communication. Communication between allopolies within an allopoly and outside of it will generally result in the loss of secrecy of the allopoly that, in turn, can result in reducing the allopoly's ability to defend itself from others, in that weaknesses are revealed. It is possible that even by simply revealing its existence, an allopoly may make itself the target of a greater number of allopolistic efforts.

E.g.: A little-known partnership found a niche as middlemen between two entire industries. The industries save money, and the partnership makes a large profit. As the individuals in the companies that comprise the industries talk about how they save money, more people discover that they can copy the partnership's business. The partnership then has competition.

It can also reduce the ability to impose allopolistic loss on other allopolies (a loss of coercive ability) or a reduction in allopolistic gain by creating a new allopoly and sharing the allopolistic gain (cooperation).

The behavior of allopolies predicted by the combined operation of *THEOREM #1: The Driving Force of Allopoly Creation*, *THEOREM #2: Allopoly Structure*, and *COROLLARY #1: Allopoly Secrecy, Cooperation, Coercion, and Force*, is clear. We have another theorem.

THEOREM #4:   Increasing Disparity in Secrecy, Coercion and Force

Allopolies will strive to increase disparities in the ability to apply force and coercion and maintain secrecy between themselves and those upon whom they would impose allopolistic loss, as well as those who may pose a threat.

Thus, as allopoly formation progresses, both allopolies within any allopoly and external allopolies will eventually attempt to protect themselves with some form of secrecy[9], at every level of allopoly formation. Allopolies will eventually protect their secrecy with coercion and force, such as imposing penalties for revealing information.

A government may also engage in secrecy by discontinuing the publication or reducing the accuracy of once-useful data that could now be used to reveal and pin-point its dysfunction.

Because the disparity in secrecy is the difference between the imposing allopoly's ability to overcome the target allopoly's ability to maintain its secrecy, the converse is also true. It is readily apparent in the perpetual conflict between individuals who want privacy (secrecy) for themselves and governments that want to eliminate it, so much so that at least one government had the protection of the individual's privacy from government intrusion as a basis.[10][11]

COROLLARY #2: Reduction of Target Allopoly Secrecy

Any given allopoly will strive to reduce secrecy of and within allopolies it attempts to control, both those it considers a current threat and those that may become a threat.

Because the ability to communicate is fundamental to the ability to maintain secrecy, apply coercion, apply force and form allopolies, *THEOREM #4: Increasing Disparity in Secrecy, Coercion and Force* has another direct corollary.

COROLLARY #3: Increasing Control of Communication

Allopolies will perpetually endeavor to increase their control of communications between allopolies and within allopolies.

It follows that when *COROLLARY #3: Increasing Control of Communication* is combined with *THEOREM #3: Preference to Form Allopolies with Governing Allopolies*, governments will increasingly take an active role in controlling communications. This is such a fundamental issue that the explicit prohibition of controlling communication was a basis of at least one government. [12] It follows that as technology develops and the number of communication methods increases, both government and private allopolies will eventually seek to control every method.

Travel

Travel generally increases the reach of communication. Therefore, as allopoly formation increases with and within governments, it follows that both government and private allopolies will attempt to control travel.

Anonymity

Anonymity is a form of secrecy and is likely the most efficient method of protecting communication and travel from being controlled. Anonymity must be removed so that a target can be identified to obtain cooperation, apply coercion or apply force per *COROLLARY #1: Allopoly Secrecy, Cooperation, Coercion, and Force*.

The combination of *THEOREM #3: Preference to Form Allopolies with Governing Allopolies*, *COROLLARY #2: Reduction of Target Allopoly Secrecy* and *COROLLARY #3: Increasing Control of Communication* predicts that government and business will actively engage in reducing and eventually eliminating the anonymity of communication and travel.

Because money is generally required for both communication and travel, these theorems also predict that both government and business allopolies will strive to eliminate the anonymity of money. This leads us directly to another corollary.

COROLLARY #4: Reduction of Anonymity

Allopolies will perpetually struggle to eliminate any means of maintaining the anonymity of money, communication and travel.

Education

During the rise of a culture, the quality and availability of education increases, thus increasing technological development that further increases the people's quality of life. Because the ability to communicate requires the ability to understand the subject under discussion, it follows that the combination of ***THEOREM #4: Increasing Disparity in Secrecy, Coercion and Force*** and ***COROLLARY #3: Increasing Control of Communication*** predicts that allopolies will eventually make efforts to reduce the education level of those upon whom they would impose allopolistic loss.[13] Because indoctrination is the most efficient method of imposing allopolistic loss, allopolists will also work to turn educational systems into indoctrination vehicles that discourage critical thinking.

COROLLARY #5: Reduction of Education Level

Because the ability to communicate is a function of the ability to understand, allopolies will strive to reduce the education level of those upon whom they impose or wish to impose allopolistic loss.

Quality of Life

Stronger allopolies achieve allopolistic gain by imposing allopolistic loss upon weaker allopolies. This inevitably results in an increasing disparity in the quality of life between the stronger and weaker allopolies. Increasing income inequality is an indicator, depicted in Figure 1 as a comparison of average and median wages.[14]

Figure 1:　　　*United States Average and Median Net Wages.*

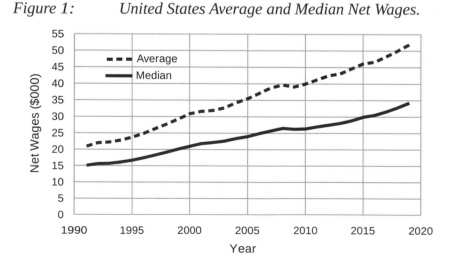

COROLLARY #6: Increasing Disparity in the Quality of Life

The imposition of allopolistic loss by one allopoly upon another allopoly increases disparity in the quality of life between allopolies.

Diffuse Acquisition and Concentrated Collection

Diffuse acquisition and concentrated collection are inherent in governments in that they collect taxes from the general population and direct those funds into the government treasury. This technique has proven irresistible as a means of imposing allopolistic loss. At least one government has created a legal process known as a class action[15] to combat it.

E.g.: A large service or utility provider with more than a million customers creates a confusing, multi-page bill that overcharges each customer one dollar every month. No individual customer will find it worth the legal expenditures, which may amount to tens of thousands of dollars plus time, in order to recoup the twelve dollars lost each year.

However, diffuse acquisition and concentrated collection are also manifested in other forms.

E.g.: Certain government employees help a private company embezzle public money. The government increases taxes to replace the lost money. The embezzlers must also pay the taxes, directly or indirectly, because they will purchase goods and services with the stolen money. The increased tax is collected in a diffuse manner from the tax-paying population, while the stolen money is concentrated in the embezzlers' hands.

E.g.: A consortium of one or more private companies forms an allopoly with lawmakers. The lawmakers pass legislation that compels all citizens to purchase a product or a service from the consortium.

E.g.:   A manufacturer deliberately does not spend the money required to make a product safe, say $10 per unit, for one single production run of 10 million units. The operation is disbanded after the production run, the equipment is moved or sold, and the warehouse is abandoned soon after all units are shipped. The product is sold in foreign countries via mail order and the internet, making it effectively impossible to sue or prosecute the individuals involved for the harm their product caused.

Whether the imposition of allopolistic loss is intended to increase the imposing allopolists' quality of life, as in the later stages of some cultures[16], or merely to maintain a certain quality of life by making up for previously imposed allopolistic loss depends upon the circumstances.

THEOREM #3: Preference to Form Allopolies with Governing Allopolies predicts that allopolies will form with and within governments. **COROLLARY #1: Allopoly Secrecy, Cooperation, Coercion, and Force** predicts these allopolies will be developed and maintained by secrecy, cooperation, coercion and force. Consequently, **COROLLARY #6: Increasing Disparity in the Quality of Life** indicates that the benefit of allopolies created with and by governments will, eventually, accrue to the allopolists at the expense of government functions.

The accumulation of allopolistic loss with and within a government can be revealed by various measures, such as an increasing inequality in the quality of life between government workers and the population and by the increasing dysfunction of the government itself.

E.g.: When a government budget crunch occurs, essential functions such as maintenance of roads, water, education, other infrastructure and services are neglected while non-essential expenditures are protected.[17]

E.g.: Control over existing, additions to, or expansions of essential infrastructure is given to for-profit organizations outside of government, as opposed to their being run by the government at cost.

E.g.: A government makes laws that give government workers more legal protections, rights, privacy and privileges than other citizens.

E.g.: A government increasingly uses its criminal justice system for revenue generation in addition to its formal tax collection. Once this process starts, because of the disparity in secrecy, coercion and force that government can impose, revenue generation will eventually come to predominate the law enforcement activity.[18] [19]

Allopoly Prevention

Governments could not be created without sufficient allegiance, or a sufficient allopoly over coercive force exercised in a manner that provides more benefit than it cost its members. In economic terms, enough people must benefit from the government to make it viable. Regardless of a government's initial form, once a government is viable, *THEOREM #1: The Driving Force of Allopoly Creation* and *THEOREM #3: Preference to Form Allopolies with Governing Allopolies* would drive the formation of allopolies.

Some governments have attempted to prevent certain types of allopoly formation among government employees.[20] Such attempts have ranged from life-time tenure, restrictions on gifts, restrictions on individual employment or that of family and associates, to prohibiting a society's military from operating within its own borders.[21] [22] Laws that would prohibit a government from disarming its populace were other attempts to prevent the formation of an allopoly, such as tyranny.[23]

Because of the amount of power achievable, virtually all allopolies seek to determine and control individuals who obtain positions of political power. Assassination is a historically ubiquitous means of preventing an individual from obtaining power or removing an individual from a position of political power. The means available to determine who attains positions of power depends upon the particulars of a government at a point in time. Elected positions are subject to election tampering efforts, which some governments resist by restricting the means to do so.[24]

Allopoly Progression

The only real difference in the progression of allopoly formation between different cultures is how long it takes for allopoly formation to capture a government's law-making arms, law enforcement arms and, ultimately, its military. One generation of allopolists will change the rules and laws of a culture for their benefit. This change is the starting point for the next generation of allopolists who make further changes to benefit themselves, and so on. Even if it takes multiple generations to dispense with the initial values of a government, that outcome will occur as long as there is local non-satiation without broad counter-incentive or opposing actions of other allopolies.

Allopoly Succession

It is clear that allopolies are not necessarily simple and may be infinite in variety. They may involve many people who would each demand a share of the allopolistic profit for their participation. Such allopolists may not have to communicate to perpetrate the conspiracy. The benefit from participating in the allopoly would be self-evident, and the meeting of the minds would occur through the action or inaction of its members. At least one country has laws to deal with such lack of collusion evidence.[25]

Both *THEOREM #1: The Driving Force of Allopoly Creation*, and *THEOREM #2: Allopoly Structure* predict that this would not be a stationary situation. Those at the top of the allopolistic pyramid would require an increase in the means of imposing their allopolistic loss to increase their allopolistic profits or expand or to defend their allopoly. They also will support the creation of allopolies with and within governing allopolies. However, the upper levels of any allopoly will need to disburse more of that power to the levels beneath them to maintain the power that can be used to impose increasing allopolistic loss. The new power realized by the lower allopoly levels will eventually be used by the lower levels for their own benefit and may ultimately depose those at the top of the allopolistic pyramids.

The process of allopoly succession may not be slow or peaceful. The manner and degrees by which those at the highest levels of the allopolistic pyramids are usurped are infinite in their variety. However, the effect of the process on society can be foreseen.

The fact that allopolies are composed of people means that the ability to maintain an allopoly is a function of how many members are loyal to it. To maintain the loyalty of locally non-satiable members at lower levels in the allopoly absent force or coercion, more benefit must be imparted to them than they could reasonably expect to gain from usurping the positions above them, including the risk involved in such an attempt. That benefit comes from the allopolistic loss that is imposed both internally and externally. This occurs at every allopoly level. One consequence is that internal allopolies attempt to secure and defend their positions.

E.g.: A new manager may attempt to protect her position by replacing her employees with others who are not as skilled or as well trained but are loyal to her. Or, a manager may try to construct a situation where he is the only person with the knowledge and experience to perform his entire job by creating a situation of high turnover of lower-skilled people who can each perform only a part of the work. In either case, the turnover is more important to the manager than training costs, learning curve mistakes and loss of organizational knowledge and institutional memory.

As allopolistic losses mount, the price of obtaining control of an allopoly increasingly requires granting allopolistic gain. As allopolistic losses accumulate, the imposition of greater allopolistic loss upon subject allopolies, and eventually the culture requires further means of imposing allopolistic loss. The specific means and methods are infinite in their variety and are categorized by **COROLLARY #1: *Allopoly Secrecy, Cooperation, Coercion, and Force***. Because allopolistic loss is increasingly imposed upon the allopolies and individuals least capable of resisting its imposition through legal means, eventually they will turn to illegal means.

A common method for the imposition of allopolistic loss is debt and usury [26], which can be a semi-permanent or permanent imposition of allopolistic loss. However, the imposition of debt on a wide scale cannot occur without government complicity.

Standards

During the rise of a culture, standards, such as in education, behavior, technology and communication, generally result in increasing competency and efficiency. With allopolistic loss accumulating on and within organizations, those organizations increasingly focus on achieving efficiencies in production, such as increased work hours, benefit reduction and elimination, lower wages, or employment loss as permanent jobs are replaced with temporary workers.

The focus on production precludes the development of new skills. The individual's reduced income and available time, in turn, reduce their opportunity to obtain an education. Thus, there is a continually decreasing ability to develop a depth and breadth of knowledge and competency, or, in other words, substance. Because this change occurs over time, it is not easily recognized except through hindsight.

As allopolies increase in size and complexity, they require a structure in which to operate. All organizations require a certain level of knowledge and skill from the individuals performing their functions.

Operational efficiencies within organizations are achieved by standardizing the organization's functions and the competencies of the individuals required to perform them. The standardization of competencies requires the definition of forms, such as educational certificates or professional licenses. The defined forms are the criteria used to replace individuals in functions over time.

The combination of a continually decreasing ability to develop depth and breadth of knowledge and competency, as well as the decreased opportunity in which to use them, results in ever-increasing importance being placed on form rather than substance as the means of advancement. This shift in the importance of form over substance results in the degradation of competency and, thus, a reduction in standards. This degradation of standards, in turn, results in operational inefficiencies, which results in further allopolistic loss being imposed upon the culture, either as a result of, or to compensate for, the loss.

E.g.: The means to obtain employment is an educational certificate. Because of the demand for this certificate, the organizations that grant them commercialize and proliferate. Competition for the educational expenditures from a population with increasingly limited means will bring with it a debasement of the actual level of education required to achieve that certificate.

E.g.: Professions requiring skill and competency (such as law, medicine, and engineering) require a certain amount of education and training. The professions are regulated to protect the public from untrained individuals practicing those professions and protect the professions themselves from commercialization and debasement. The regulatory methods used range from apprenticeship programs and professional licensing to limiting the ownership and control of businesses that engage in that profession to only those professionals. [27] [28]

However, there is no imputed morality for individuals in the professions who will create allopolies to increase their own gain. If the regulated professions are necessary for a society, such as law or medicine, the increasing costs may make the professional services unobtainable by the average person. The result may be attempts to create competition in the profession.[29]

Eventually, professional standards will degrade, and the prohibitions on ownership of a professional business by non-professionals will erode. Then, allopolies of untrained and unskilled non-professionals compromise the professions for commercial gain by virtue of being the supervisors of the professionals or indirectly by deciding the specific acts for which the professional will be paid.

Values

The general values of a rising culture are associated with lower levels of imposed allopolistic loss, compared to its decline when prevailing values are associated with higher levels of imposed allopolistic loss. As allopolistic losses accumulate, *COROLLARY #6: Increasing Disparity in the Quality of Life* predicts that the disparity in the quality of life will increase.

As the quality-of-life disparity increases, those with reduced circumstances will have decreasing opportunities for creating allopolies and for resisting or compensating for the imposition of allopolistic loss upon themselves. They must spend increasing amounts of their resources simply to maintain their quality of life. Accordingly, their ability to plan and act for the long-term decreases. Thus, over time, the culture's values shift toward seeking actions that pay off in the increasingly shorter term.

COROLLARY #7: Value Shift from Long to Short Term

As allopolistic losses mount in a culture, form becomes more important than substance, and the general outlook of the culture's actions increasingly shifts from the long term to the short term.

Eventually, one's previous quality of life cannot be maintained. As the individual's quality of life decreases due to the accumulation of imposed allopolistic loss, their endeavors become focused on maintaining their own lifestyle at the expense of other values. Where once carpenters and builders employed flourishes and style, construction and architecture progressively become more utilitarian.[26] The pride people once took in their work decreases over time until none remains.

Cascading Allopolistic Loss due to Dishonesty

As the quality of life decreases, the incidence and level of dishonesty can be expected to increase due to its initial low cost. Further, it can also be expected that collusion, which also has a low initial cost, will follow.

Increasing dishonesty imposes its own allopolistic losses beyond what might be attained through dishonesty directly. As dishonesty increases, so does the need to expend resources to verify honesty. The allopolistic losses imposed by the increase in dishonesty are the costs of verification, the opportunities forgone due to avoidance of verification costs, and the losses due to intended acts of the dishonest.

Rule and Law Violations and Changes

Many laws, such as those dealing with violence against one's person and the theft or damage to the property of another, are designed to limit the imposition of allopolistic loss upon others. To be one of the few law breakers can yield allopolistic gains not available to individuals or allopolies that do not break the law.

The ever-present allure of the gain from breaking the rules exists for individuals, organizations, businesses, governments, and any other form of allopoly. The differences are in how such policies are broken, enforced or changed over time. Dishonesty can reduce the risk and penalties for rule-breakers, and collusion can further lessen them.

Allopoly analysis suggests two general categories explaining why an allopolist may break a rule: To change their ability to create or join allopolies and/or to change their level of allopolistic gain. Here, "change" describes an increase or decrease, or the prevention thereof.

It can generally be inferred that the rule-breaker assumes that their action will not have negative consequences if they can get away with it. The other implicit assumption is that the number of people breaking that rule is too small to affect the rule-breaker.

E.g.: A robber does not expect to be robbed on the way home from a robbery, but she is robbed by a masked man. He, in turn, does not expect to be robbed on his way home from robbing the robber, but is, and so on.

Changes to rules come in many forms, such as the selective enforcement of penalties for the violation of existing rules or changes to the existing rules that give a particular allopoly an advantage. Thus, if a rule is changed or a law is written in a manner that benefits only a particular allopoly at the expense of others, it is not considered breaking a rule or law. However, such an action still constitutes the imposition of allopolistic loss.

To a system outsider, allopolistic activities may be difficult to perceive or measure due to the inherent lack of available information on prohibited or illegal actions. However, in cultures with written laws, records could show changes in the enforcement of laws or even changes in the written laws themselves. Such would be evidenced by a progression of changes in the written laws that gave increasing favor to those with allopolies with government, possibly along with increasing disregard for the long-term consequences.

E.g.: Fresh drinking water is an irreplaceable staple of life, yet a government permits private interests to permanently poison the aquifers from whence the drinking water comes for the short-term profits of the private interests and those within the government who are part of the allopoly. This occurs even though poisoning drinking water would normally be considered an act of war or terrorism.

Would this result be limited to governments alone?
THEOREM #1: The Driving Force of Allopoly Creation, and
THEOREM #3: Preference to Form Allopolies with Governing Allopolies have already answered this question in the negative. This result would occur in every organization of people that has a governing hierarchy. In business associations, managers at every level will hire and promote individuals loyal to them but not necessarily to the organization. The decisions of such managers will increasingly be made to improve their own quality of life. The creation of further allopolies with other control functions within an organization will result in an even greater quality of life for the allopolists within the organization, imposed as allopolistic loss on the organization as a whole.

As applied to an organization, **COROLLARY #7: *Value Shift from Long to Short Term*** predicts that the shift to short-term payoffs would come at the expense of long-term strategy. As the focus of the controlling allopoly shifts from the long-term strategy that most benefits the organization toward shorter-term strategies that benefit the allopolists within the organization, eventually, the allopolistic loss imposed on the organization will grow to outweigh the allopolist's contribution to the organization.

Putting these drivers together, we see that because of the accumulation of allopolistic loss, there is an increasing incentive for individuals to shift their outlook from longer to shorter terms, to be dishonest and engage in conspiracies.

Technology

The focus shift from long term to short term manifests itself in the pursuit of more immediate concrete returns, such as cash payoffs or appointments to positions as opposed to long-term investments with returns not immediately realized, such as education and infrastructure. Combined with the shift in the importance of form over substance, the shift from long-term to short-term outlooks will adversely affect the areas of a society that require long-term planning and investment.

One example is basic research, which is typically undertaken to learn without expectation of return on the investment in the foreseeable future. However, basic research often leads to applied research, which uses basic research results with an expectation of returns on the investment.[30] [31]

The objective measure through which this process can be seen is a decline in the rate of technological advancement that is propagated over time. In particular, the nature of innovation will shift from **radical** or **discontinuous**, which is the result of a totally new innovation such as the invention of transistors, to **incremental** innovation, which is the refinement of an existing technology. The reason for the shift is that the investment risk of developing a radical technology that has not been done before is greater than that of making relatively minor changes to an existing technology.

Technological advancement generally reduces the amount of resources required to achieve some purpose or makes it possible. This reduced cost is a benefit that can be realized from an individual level up to that of the entire culture, depending on the advancement and its dispersion. In this sense, technological advancement offsets increasing allopolistic loss.

With a reduction in the offset of increasing allopolistic loss due to the slowdown in technological advancement, **THEOREM #1: The Driving Force of Allopoly Creation** predicts that allopolistic endeavors will then focus on extracting allopolistic gain from existing technologies and allopolies, thereby imposing allopolistic loss on the very functions that produce the technological advancements and thus further slowing technological development. Thus **COROLLARY #7: Value Shift from Long to Short Term**, in part explains why the peak of a civilization's technological development precedes its demise.[32]

Technology such as communications, surveillance and weapons can be used to both impose and resist the imposition of allopolistic loss. So, too, can growing reliance upon a technology that is then restricted or withheld.[33]

Foreseeable End

Allopolies in the form of business associations are created to consolidate allopolistic power. One form of business association is nothing more than a piece of paper that represents the financial interests of those who formed the allopoly. This form is called a corporation. Its structure creates an allopoly that limits control of the owners, the shareholders, and at the same time protects them from legal liability for the corporation's actions. Because a piece of paper is immune to death, and therefore never suffers the dissipating effect of inheritance issues or even legal issues, as pieces of paper are not sentenced to prison terms, these allopolies can amass great wealth within a few short generations. At least one country has enacted laws designed to limit the ability of corporations to form allopolies.[34] *THEOREM #1: The Driving Force of Allopoly Creation* predicted that allopolies would form within the corporation allopoly. Such could be evidenced by the continual changes of the rules by which they operate[35], and is borne out by the continual machinations and power struggles within them.

It is predicted by *THEOREM #3: Preference to Form Allopolies with Governing Allopolies*, that the allopolies of any organization outside of government would strive to make allopolies with governments, and those within governments. This activity can be evidenced by a continual erosion of restrictions on the interactions of government and private interests. Examples include employment of a government employee and their family or legalizing the dispersion of unlimited funds to those seeking elected government positions.[36] [37]

The owners of a corporation, the shareholders, have every interest in tying the benefits conferred to hired management directly to the results of their decisions. Those decisions will affect the health of the business in the long term. Some industries have attempted to link compensation to the results of decisions in the longer term.[38] However, there is less risk for the allopolies in control of corporations, that is the hired management, if they can obtain their bonuses before the results of their decisions can be fully measured.

COROLLARY #6: Increasing Disparity in the Quality of Life predicts that those not in the allopoly in control of the corporation will suffer allopolistic loss. With the long-term results of managers' decisions decoupled from their benefits, those benefits will increase.[39]

First, the owners (shareholders) lose as corporate profits are reduced, or the corporation may even go out of business. One indication this is occurring would be that bonuses and other compensation remain high while owner profits in the form of dividends, dwindle or disappear.

Another indicator are workers, who had been persuaded to invest in the company by deferring their compensation through investment and who leveraged interest earnings by waiting 25 years for pensions, suffer a loss as the pensions are systematically underfunded to increase management's own short-term gains. In this manner, the hired management, the allopoly in control of the corporation, can take its allopolistic gain for themselves and impose the loss upon the owners and workers.

Allopoly versus Culture

At what point does the taking turn those taken from into slaves?

As the accumulation of allopolistic loss upon a culture increases, it will eventually exceed the allopolistic gain the culture's allopolies can provide their allopolists. This will mark the beginning of the unraveling of an allopolistic structure. Whether the parts are joined into other allopolies or create smaller, more sustainable allopolies will depend upon the circumstances.

At one extreme, a civil war may take place where the opposing sides (allopolies) formed within the larger allopoly (country) attempt to break away. Another extreme would be taking over the country by ousting the current allopoly leadership in a coup d'état. Yet another example is the overthrow of a regime by revolution (creating a new allopoly) using the promise of reducing the allopolistic loss imposed by the old regime as a recruitment incentive. There is an infinite number of variations, including the breaking up and dissolution of an entire empire.

The breakdown of a civilization will probably follow a path that adheres to the lines of degradation of government functions. It will continue to break down into successively smaller allopolies, to towns, villages, families and individuals if need be, until it is again advantageous for larger groups of people to work together for their common benefit.

In the time frame of civilizations (hundreds of years), there has not been a single culture or civilization that has not followed a cycle of growth and decay, as evidenced by the lack of a single continuous arc of education and technological development throughout history.[32] Some societies have been able to control the growth of allopolistic pyramids longer than others by virtue of strong family leadership, such as an emperor. Nevertheless, dynastic cultures have crumbled with subsequent generations, as have cultures that have changed due to revolutions by those subject to tyranny.

Conquest and the extraction of economic gain from outside one group would feed the conquering society's ever-growing allopolistic pyramids by providing a surplus greater than the current allopolistic loss, albeit at the expense of the conquered group.[26] However, this would be only a temporary offset in terms of the economic benefits and, in the case of war, a possible lowering of the intensity of allopolistic drivers by decreasing the population. Allopolistic losses would continue to mount until the culture could no longer support it. That is, the desire to undermine or even abandon an allopolistic structure would become increasingly widespread.

However, allopolistic loss is not a single value imposed by a given allopolist. Individuals and allopolies will resist the imposition of loss. This defensive effort is an expense that is also part and parcel of the loss imposed upon a culture by the allopolists. If the imposition cannot be resisted, it may be mitigated by other efforts, including recovery by the imposition of that loss upon other allopolies, if possible.

E.g.: The business and property taxes of a neighborhood grocery store increase. To maintain its profit at the same level before the tax increase, the grocery store owner raises his prices. He does not raise the prices on goods with high demand elasticity, that is, items for which the demand is tightly linked to price because the demand for those goods would decrease. Instead, the grocer raises the prices of items with low demand elasticity, that is, staples.

Each customer will then have to pay more for staples until the prices match or exceed the combined cost of transportation and the opportunity cost of the customer's time to shop at a grocery store with lower prices. The result is that the customer's quality of life is lowered. A particular customer's circumstances will determine what actions they take to maintain their quality of life. Some acts, such as theft, may, in turn, impose allopolistic loss upon others and so on.

Thus there are both multiplicative and cascading effects of the loss imposed by allopolies that force efforts and resources to be expended by yet other allopolies, and so on. Imposed allopolistic losses need not be monetary.

COROLLARY #8: Multiplicative and Cascade Effect of Allopolistic Loss

The accumulation of allopolistic loss is caused by both the locally non-satiable individual's attempts to improve or maintain their quality of life by imposing losses on others, and the resources expended by individuals and allopolies to prevent or mitigate the imposition of allopolistic loss upon themselves.

Law

Legal systems are the creation of governments and cultures that make up civilizations. The primary purpose of a legal system depends on the current state of a government with respect to its allopoly progression and the imposition of allopolistic loss. A government that is relatively free of allopolistic loss will have a legal system that reduces the imposition of allopolistic loss upon its citizens. A tyrannical government will have a high degree of allopolistic loss and will use its legal system as a means to impose allopolistic loss upon its citizens, reduce the citizen's ability to defend themselves from this imposition and direct that allopolistic gain to specific allopolies, namely the tyrants.

The Cycle of Civilization

The rise and fall of a civilization is actually a cycle, which is a surprising result. More importantly, we have discovered what is behind the cycle of civilization: Allopolistic activity.

THEOREM #1: The Driving Force of Allopoly Creation, predicts that allopolies will be formed within larger allopolies. *THEOREM #4: Increasing Disparity in Secrecy, Coercion and Force* predicts that allopolies, at any level, will attempt to protect their position by decreasing the ability of other allopolies to challenge them. Generally speaking, the power of any allopoly in any organization is a function of time in position and the number of members loyal to the allopoly. One effective way to seize power is to remove all the individuals who are not loyal to the allopoly within an organization, as opposed to those loyal to the organization.

THEOREM #2: Allopoly Structure predicts that allopolies will have a pyramid structure. Allopolies below the level of the newly arriving controlling allopolist are at risk of being replaced. This replacement will occur at every allopoly level. With increasing turnover, the ability to obtain long-term benefits from an allopoly disappears. As the ability to make long term gains from an allopoly decreases, the culture's values will shift from the long term to obtaining benefits in the short term. In turn this increases the allopolistic-loss imposition rate.

A key point is that it is not necessarily a single allopoly that determines the total imposition of allopolistic loss. Because it is the governing structures themselves that impose or permit the imposition of allopolistic loss on the culture, an analogy can be made to the Tragedy of the Commons[40], wherein farmers share a communal pasture to graze their sheep. Each farmer thinks that one additional sheep will not cause any harm. However, if enough farmers graze enough additional sheep, the capacity of the commons will be exceeded, and all the sheep will starve. The analogy becomes complete when the farmers' outlook is shortened to only feeding their sheep today, with no regard for what may come tomorrow.

As long as individuals are locally non-satiable, and there is more perceived benefit to allopoly formation than not, allopoly formation will progress. Therefore, it is not possible to create an enduring culture without altering these motivations.

THEOREM #5:   The Driving Force Behind the Cycle of Civilization

The Cycle of Civilization will repeat as long as individuals exhibit local non-satiation and their ability to impose allopolistic loss upon others is not impeded.

Given the infinite variety of possible allopolies, as long as individuals exhibit local non-satiation and there is a probability in any given amount of time that humans could form allopolies beneficial to themselves, they will do so. Changing that probability and/or the payoff of the allopoly will succeed only in changing the amount of time required for the rise of allopoly formation and its eventual dominance.

> *What mechanism permits the cycle of civilization to begin, without individuals creating allopolies that preempt its formation?*

In the mining example, the miners saw how they could have a productive mine. The government they formed with their children as police was both visible to, and near them, as were the negatives of the bandits. However, the visibility of the bandits would disappear with subsequent generations who did not live through it. The visibility and attainability of the loyal police force would disappear as the population grew and the functions of government became more distant, even invisible. The combination of visibility and attainability was a key mechanism.

Although the economics of cooperation are straightforward, cooperation would not occur if individuals sought shorter-term gains through the imposition of allopolistic loss upon others.

E.g.: Two people could not cooperate to plant a crop if one of the people stole the tools (hoe, plow, horse) and sold them for cash.

Therefore, a shared longer-term outlook or a weakening of the disparity of some factors identified in ***COROLLARY #1: Allopoly Secrecy, Cooperation, Coercion, and Force*** between allopolists and those upon whom they would impose their allopolistic loss was what permitted the formation of allopolies that provided more benefit than loss. A shared outlook answers the apparent riddle of allopoly formation and civilization.

THEOREM #6: The Riddle of Allopoly Formation and Civilization

While allopoly formation will not necessarily lead to the creation of a civilization, a civilization cannot be created without the formation of allopolies. At the same time, it is the accumulation of allopolistic loss imposed by allopolies upon a civilization that destroys it.

This riddle is a staggeringly complex problem involving the population of an entire civilization and the infinite number of allopoly variations that could and will form.

Is it even possible to develop a code of rules to prevent allopoly formation from destroying a culture or a civilization?

No, it is not. Because the allopoly variation is infinite, so too would have to be any code of rules addressing the creation of individual allopolies.

Although allopolies are the source of the problem, they are not in themselves the problem, per se. Therefore, the solution to the problem cannot be found at the level of the problem, which is allopoly creation. The problem is caused by the allopolistic loss that allopolies impose upon others. We should look for the answer in the imposition of allopolistic loss.

Measurement

Back to the original question: What is slavery?

We can now see that slavery is, in fact, a type of allopoly. According to our definition of allopoly, the act of enslavement is the imposition of allopolistic loss leaving the individual no recourse. However, in practice, allopolies are difficult to see. Attempting to identify all the allopolies within any structure greater than a tiny village is nearly impossible. Generally, only monetary costs are visible. Even then, accounting tricks may hide all but the most blatant of allopolistic losses. Such difficulties impede the definition of slavery in clear and objective terms.

To arrive at a definition of slavery, we need a visible, objective metric that will quantify allopolistic loss. With such a measure, it would not matter what form the allopoly took, for the imposition of the allopolistic loss could be directly measured and acted on. Without such a measure, creating an economy in the earlier example of the wide valley populated by farmers and artisans would be no different from creating another situation that, given the drivers of allopoly creation, would eventually have allopolies develop that strive to impose allopolistic loss on its population.

We must also use that measure to find a clear point that would define the specific point when the allopolists turned the population into slaves. That point cannot be arbitrary, but must arise naturally from the metric itself to be a valid, unbiased measure.

Definitions of slavery have varied throughout history. Some said it was the opposite of freedom. Others would say it was whatever the law defined as slavery. Those laws were written by the allopolists who did the enslaving. If the term "slavery" were to have negative effects on the allopolists, then the laws would be written so that the definition of slavery would fall just outside the allopolists' activities. The fact that "slavery" was given another name would be of little consolation to the slaves, whose situation would not change.

A measure of slavery is needed that does not depend upon subjective and ever-changing perceptions, definitions and laws. People make definitions and perceive, and governments make laws. The measure must be applicable to all individuals and all governments to be independent of perceptions, definitions and laws.

Currency is the metric predominantly used in economic analysis. Using money as a metric greatly simplifies economic analysis, but it also conceals a great deal[41] and can misdirect economic analysis. Furthermore, the value of currency fluctuates over time and may be manipulated.

A precise metric will be impervious to such manipulation. An accurate metric would not fluctuate over time.

Time as an Economic Measure

Time is the key. Everything to do with an economy affects the time of any individual. The value of currency fluctuates. The value of goods fluctuates. The value of labor fluctuates. But the value of time to the individual does not. Everyone's time is the same from their perspective. We have an objective metric: Time.

THEOREM #7:   Time as an Economic Measure

The time of an individual is directly measurable. Time is the same from the perspective of all individuals. Time is not affected by definitions, and almost everything to do with an economy affects an individual's time. Therefore, time is the single best economic measure for the individual.

Now we must apply the time metric to the two examples used to reach this point, and see what changes.

EXAMPLE #3:   The Robber (using time as a measure)

A couple had amassed objects of a certain monetary value that increased the quality of their lives. The process of amassing them had taken the couple's time. At the point of a gun, the robber increased his quality of life by taking from the couple the time they had invested in acquiring what he took from them. The robber thus received more time than he spent in the allopolistic endeavor to get it.

Regardless of whether the robber stole goods or currency, what actually occurred was the exchange of the results of one person's time for the results of another person's time. The difference between the robbery and forcing the couple to work their entire lives to obtain the goods he stole, is the amount of time the robber expended to obtain them.

At its best, money makes an exchange easier by eliminating the double-coincidence requirement of barter. Money could become a means of storing people's time. However, while money might represent an accumulation of time, it also might not, such as in the case of inflation and deflation. The use of time as a metric eliminates the variability in the value of money.

THEOREM #8:   Goods and Services are Accumulations of Time. Absent Fluctuations in its Value so is Money

Goods and services represent the accumulation of the time of the individuals who create or provide them. Absent significant fluctuations in its value, money can represent accumulations of time.

What about resources? Even in the event of the absolute control of resources, if no one were willing to exchange their time for those resources, they would have little value. One would have to make a distinction between resources that preclude the imposition of allopolistic loss, and those that do not.

E.g.: A tract of land would have little value to the allopolist who controlled it if the time of others could not be exchanged for its use or for something it produced. The exception would be if living on the land meant the allopolist did not have to purchase or rent other land on which to live.

This leads us to the objective of an allopoly.

THEOREM #9:   The Objective of an Allopoly

The objective of an allopoly is to control their own time and resources, and the time and resources of others for the benefit of those within the allopoly.

The combination of *THEOREM #1: The Driving Force of Allopoly Creation*, *THEOREM #2: Allopoly Structure* and *THEOREM #3: Preference to Form Allopolies with Governing Allopolies* predicts that the forces that drive the cycle of civilization will eventually result in allopolistic pyramids being formed both with and within government. Now, it becomes clear that allopolistic loss is imposed in the form of time on other allopolies, whether it is forcing individuals and other allopolies to give up their time by working, taking the results of their accumulated time by confiscating their possessions and savings or by taking away their ability to defend their allopolies or make new ones, thus limiting the use of their future time.

THEOREM #10: Measurement of Allopolistic Loss

Allopolistic loss is the direct or indirect taking of resources and time by one allopoly from other allopolies.

Time, Culture, Education and Technology

Using time as a metric also provides a different perspective on the value of a culture's or civilization's technological development. A particular item represents more than just the time spent by individuals to create it. It also represents the time spent in acquiring the tools and resources used to make the item. It further represents the historical time spent by the culture in developing the necessary societal stability and technology that enabled its creation. The same accounting logic applies to the skills used to provide a service.

THEOREM #11: Measurement Basis for Social and Technological Development

The social and technological development of a civilization is a historical accumulation of time upon which the time of an individual is leveraged.

At first glance, this historical time cost represents an astronomical change to the cost of an item or a service. It includes all the decades and centuries spent building a society, including the total time lost in wars to defend it.

In any trade or sale at a particular point in time within a given culture, this historical time cost will generally cancel because all the individuals from the same culture are under the same historical time cost. However, a trade of items or services between individuals of different cultures would involve the differences between the historical time each culture had invested in its development.

E.g.:   Technologically advanced Culture A, which possesses antibiotics, could sell their medical services to a more primitive Culture B that did not have such a high level of medical technology for more time than those services could be sold to Culture A.

E.g.: If technologically advanced Culture A taught primitive Culture B its technology, then Culture A effectively gave away its entire historical investment and advantage to Culture B, which can now compete on an equal footing without the investment of time to reach that point.

In the robber example, the couple's possessions may have more value to the robber if the robber came from a primitive culture and the couple was from a more advanced culture. The reverse would generally be true as well. Now we must test the mining example using time as a measure.

EXAMPLE #4:   The Miners (using time as a measure)

The miners invested their time to acquire knowledge and tools. They also invested time to discover the mine and extract the copper, process it and turn it into the goods they sold to increase the quality of their lives.

The bandits arrived and, with an allopoly on force, obtained all of the miners' time: their current time spent laboring on that day, time spent on subsequent days under control of the bandits and all the time the miners had previously invested.

When the miners' children grew up, they overpowered the bandits, taking away their allopoly on force.

The miners hired some of the children as a police force to protect them against other bandits.

Although the miners regained control of their time, the amount of time the miners could spend to improve their quality of life is less than it was before the bandits arrived. The difference is what they must pay to support their police force, that is, part of their government.

Before the bandits arrived, the miners had invested their time into developing and acquiring the technology of copper mining. When the bandits imposed their allopoly of force upon the miners' allopoly of the mine, the bandits took all the miners' time by forcing them to work by day and then throwing them into cages at night. In this situation, one reason the miners could not further develop their technology was that they had no time to do it.

By extension, a culture that lives at a subsistence level and spends all its time obtaining shelter and food will have a very slow technological development. A culture that devotes a great deal of time to the advancement of technology will likely develop technology faster. Thus, technological development will have a fundamental relationship to the education level of those spending time advancing technology.

E.g.: In the same culture, the time spent by an illiterate, uneducated person in advancing the level of technology will likely yield less technological advancement than would the same amount of time spent by a person with the same intelligence who was educated in the sciences.

However, education alone is not the sole determining factor for the differences in the rate of technological advancement. That rate is also related to the number of individuals, their level of intellect and thought processes.

E.g.: An individual of higher than average intelligence who is uneducated and illiterate, will likely produce less technological advancement than several million educated individuals of average intelligence, with each spending the same amount of time in the advancement of technology.

THEOREM #12: Rate of a Civilization's Technological Development

The rate of a civilization's technological development is a function of the amount of time spent developing its technology, the educational level, the experience and intellect of the individuals doing so.

Many civilizations begin with an increasing rate of technological development. Agriculture, which replaced hunting and gathering as the primary food source, required less labor to feed the same number of individuals and was also a more stable food source. In turn, this relative abundance and stability made more time available to advance science and, subsequently, technology. The improved science and technology in turn freed up more labor, and so on.[42]

The incidence of genius can be negated by the lack of education. By genius it is meant individuals at the upper-end of the intelligence spectrum. Education represents a large historical quantity of time investment that frees the individual from repeating the same work and making the same discoveries (or mistakes) as their forebears. Instead, the individual can spend time advancing the level of technology by building upon its current level. This leads directly to the value of an education.

THEOREM #13: Education and Time

An education builds upon what has already been learned. Thus it is an accumulation of time that permits the individual to benefit from the time investment that previous generations, cultures and even entire civilizations have made in acquiring knowledge.

As long as the combination of the incidence of genius, upbringing and opportunity for education is probabilistic, the best way to gain the advantage of genius is to educate the greatest number of people. This yields a direct corollary regarding the number of educated people.

COROLLARY #9:   Technological Advancement Versus the Number of Educated Individuals

Given the same intelligence level, the same educational level, the same experience and the same amount of time spent by each individual in the advancement of a culture's technology, a significantly larger number of people will generally yield more technological advancement than a significantly smaller number of people. Furthermore, the greater the size of the educated population, the greater the chance of educating a genius.

In some cases when civilizations fell, others picked up their technology. In other cases, technology was lost and had to be reinvented. The circumstances for the varying degrees of technological retention between cultures and civilizations follow directly from *THEOREM #13: Education and Time* and *COROLLARY #9: Technological Advancement Versus the Number of Educated Individuals*.

COROLLARY #10: Continuity of a Level of Technology

To be able to maintain a technology at a given level, the requisite education must be imparted to succeeding generations in sufficient numbers to both maintain the technology and impart the education of the technological level to successive generations.

No single reason explains why there has not been a continuous evolution of technology. Instead, many different civilizations have fallen, and their technology was lost.[43] A better explanation for the decline in the rate of technological advancement that generally precedes the decline of a civilization is a combination of *THEOREM #12: Rate of a Civilization's Technological Development*, *THEOREM #13: Education and Time*, *COROLLARY #5: Reduction of Education Level*, *COROLLARY #7: Value Shift from Long to Short Term*,

COROLLARY #9: Technological Advancement Versus the Number of Educated Individuals, and *COROLLARY #10: Continuity of a Level of Technology*, which suggests that multiple effects and their interactions are responsible. Putting them all together yields another corollary.

COROLLARY #11: The Arc of a Culture's Technological Advancement

Given any culture-wide technological achievement, the accumulation of allopolistic loss causes a shift in cultural values from the long term to the short term. The shorter the outlook of the culture, the fewer people spending time performing basic research, from which springs applied research.

Allopolies will eventually strive to reduce the education level of those upon whom they impose allopolistic loss, that is, the general population.

The large-scale lowering of the education level reduces the value of the stored time the culture's knowledge represents. The culture must then engage in reinvention. This reinvention cost is repeatedly imposed in all the fields that support technology.

As reinvention costs mount, the point is eventually reached at which all the available time and resources are expended merely to reach a previous level of technology, rendering any radical technological advancements, that is, completely new and different inventions, increasingly unlikely. Technological advancement increasingly becomes limited to the more certain and immediate return on the investment of applied research, that is, incremental technological advancements upon what is already known.

As the rate of technological advancement slows, the culture increasingly directs its efforts into creating and maintaining allopolies on current technologies and eventually even stops efforts in applied research.

Ultimately, technological advancement effectively comes to a halt. Thus, technological advancement reaches a peak and declines before the demise of a civilization. This is part of the cycle of civilization.

Analytical Implications

Implicit in the preceding was what could appear to be irrational behavior analyzed solely on a monetary basis. However, the use of time as a metric and the perceived ability to defend and create allopolies may explain such behavior even if they were not calculable due to the infinite variety of situations possible. As long as allopoly formation and the imposition of allopolistic loss occur, the behavior would also occur.

Using time as the metric for allopolistic loss gives a different perspective on many interactions. Attempts to gain status and prestige within a society are actually efforts to gain an allopoly over the time of others.

For humans, this starts early in life, as children vie for the attention, that is, the time of their parents, teachers and peers. However, the difficulty in measuring unquantifiable but perceived real pay-offs for actions has analytical implications.

The prisoner's dilemma is a basic game theory exercise based upon rational expectations in which all the information is available.[44] However, game theory is not so easily applied when payoff information is not available or may not exist at all.[45]

The individual's consideration of allopoly formation that may lead to further opportunity for allopoly resistance or creation, combined with their perception and weighting of the information available to them at the moment, may drive individuals to take actions that appear irrational on a monetary basis. The value of status symbols in the social process of allopoly formation explains the existence of Veblen goods[46], which are high quality or luxury goods for which the demand increases with price increases.

COROLLARY #12: Game Theory

What may appear as irrational behavior by a rational locally non-satiable individual may, in fact, be rational behavior when using time as the metric, by taking into account the individual's perception of the change in their ability to form allopolies, or the change in their ability to resist the imposition of allopolistic loss.

Non-Government Allopolies

Private businesses are another example of allopolies. The larger the business, the less visible the operations to others within it, both laterally and vertically. Businesses will seek to form allopolies in which they are the sole provider of products and services. Left unchecked, this behavior can lead to complete control of services and products by one allopoly. An allopoly can be a single individual, a single company or a cartel of cooperating allopolies.

However, businesses have a form of internal control over allopolistic development and progression. That is, absent acquiring the power of law to protect them, businesses need at the very least, to break even.

Government Allopolies

The function of government was developed from the ground up in *EXAMPLE #1: The Robber*, and *EXAMPLE #2: The Miners*. This progression represents a possible early stage of government, where it imparts more benefit than it costs.

However, government allopolies are substantially different once the imposition of allopolistic loss, including direct and indirect taxes and costs, exceeds the benefits provided by the government. That would logically be the point at which an individual becomes a slave.

From one perspective, a government can be viewed as an allopoly in a constant state of bailout in the form of taxes. Government allopolies do not need to be profitable. Allopoly progression is only checked by specific laws, and then only if such laws are enforced. Law enforcement becomes less likely if the government workers who are supposed to enforce the laws are also those who benefit by breaking them. With respect to **COROLLARY #1: Allopoly Secrecy, Cooperation, Coercion, and Force**, governments have the law on their side.

E.g.: A government runs a supermarket. The manager decides that career advancement will be determined by the winners of weekly food fights in the store. The manager reports the resulting food loss as spoilage. The manager also fires employees who threaten to report the manager to higher authorities. Only individuals who would not report the matter to higher authorities are hired. With a continual influx of taxes to make up for the losses, managers are free to focus on developing their own allopolies.

Corruption

One definition of corruption is "dishonest or illegal behavior especially by powerful people (such as government officials or police officers): depravity". Another definition is "a departure from the original or from what is pure or correct".[47] However, in the context of allopoly theory, *corruption* has one meaning irrespective of morality or legality. An allopoly becomes corrupt when it obtains allopolistic gain in a manner that is not part of its intended function. All allopolies are subject to corruption as it is their mode of incentivization.

In private business allopolies, corruption can continue only to the point that the allopolistic loss imposed upon the business from internal allopolies and external allopolies exceeds the business profits resulting in bankruptcy.

Government corruption is a different matter for two reasons. First, governments generally do not have the same limitations on the accumulation of allopolistic loss that the profit requirement imposes on private businesses.

Second, governments generally have greater legal protections. These protections are, in essence, legal shields provided by lawmakers to protect the government and government employees. These protections range from immunity from legal recourse to onerous processes and impediments to legal recourse. When a government becomes corrupt, it increasingly turns those shields into swords.

E.g.: One tenet of a government is the right of its citizens to redress. A corrupt government wishes to reduce the ability of its citizens to access redress without appearing to do so. This government places caps on what may be awarded in lawsuits. These caps are near the cost of bringing the suit against the government, thereby reducing the incentive and ability to pursue legal recourse. The government has thus subverted one of its founding principles.

Oversight

Ostensibly, the purpose of oversight is to prevent the corruption of an organization. To function, the overseer becomes the highest level of the organization being overseen. Oversight organizations can foster corruption by both action and inaction. Inaction can grant the overseer a level of protection from a legal system by using the concept of plausible deniability and then calling for a "special task force" to do what was originally the overseer's job.

E.g.: A department is responsible for overseeing the shipments in and out of a storage facility. The department manager assists in the theft of laptop computers by not fixing an insecure warehouse door and a hole in the fence. After the loss is discovered the manager claims ignorance of the needed repairs and calls for a special task force to stop the disappearance of laptops. The task force recommends the appropriate repairs. The supervisor who hired the manager defends her own judgment by giving the manager an award for the work with the task force.

By determining what rules will be scrutinized and what rules will be ignored, the overseer effectively sets policy. Thus, individuals working at even low levels of the overseer's organization are defacto policy makers.

Once the top level of an organization becomes corrupt, it is only a question of time before all the levels of its management become corrupt or are replaced with corrupt individuals. As this occurs, the oversight organization's workers either become corrupt or are forced out. This situation is exacerbated when the oversight organization itself lacks substantive independent oversight.

Draining the Swamp

In simple terms, if an organization has become so corrupt that it is a swamp in need of draining, then it is the overseers who have become the plugs in the drain.

This outcome is predicted by *THEOREM #3: Preference to Form Allopolies with Governing Allopolies*. The organizations with oversight functions will be the more desirable allopoly-formation targets.

Organizations with oversight functions have authority over the organizations they oversee, per *THEOREM #4: Increasing Disparity in Secrecy, Coercion and Force* and *COROLLARY #2: Reduction of Target Allopoly Secrecy*. Thus, it is unreasonable not to expect allopoly formation with and within an oversight organization.

The more drivers of allopoly formation in operation and the greater their intensity, the more likely there will eventually be corruption, regardless of what allopoly is being overseen. The following illustrations show how allopoly formation might turn into corruption of not only the overseer, but of the organization they oversee.

E.g.: An Office of Inspector General exists at most government agencies in the United States government. The purpose is to oversee the particular agency to prevent fraud, waste and abuse. By law each Office of Inspector General has an Office of Audit and an Office of Investigations (law enforcement). The Offices of Inspectors General are the overseers of the United States government.

All Offices of Inspectors General are independent of each other and the agency they oversee. There is no substantive independent oversight of the Offices of Inspectors General themselves.

In terms of allopoly drivers, each Office of Inspector General starts with **THEOREM #1: The Driving Force of Allopoly Creation**, as do all allopolies. However, because of its position, the following drivers are both in place and amplified: **THEOREM #3: Preference to Form Allopolies with Governing Allopolies**, **COROLLARY #1: Allopoly Secrecy, Cooperation, Coercion, and Force** and **COROLLARY #2: Reduction of Target Allopoly Secrecy**. Because an Office of Inspector General has no substantive independent oversight, the effect of **THEOREM #4: Increasing Disparity in Secrecy, Coercion and Force** is highly amplified. In this situation the effect of dishonesty is also amplified. In combination with collusion, dishonesty becomes a potent weapon and threat against any single individual, both inside and outside the Office of Inspector General.

United States federal employees take an oath when becoming government workers. That oath is to defend the United States Constitution, not the particular organization or patronage in which they work.

If an Office of Inspector General becomes corrupt, it can easily end the career of one of its employees for not colluding in the corruption. The government worker may face a choice between keeping their oath to defend the United States Constitution, then being forced out of their job and not be able to provide for their families. Or, they may tacitly collude with the corruption, thereby giving the corrupt management actual leverage to use against them instead of threats and false accusations.

Because there is no substantive independent oversight of an Office of Inspector General, there is very little that can be done if corruption sets in. Absent hard evidence of corruption, the most that a sitting United States president may do is remove the person at the top of the organization, the inspector general.[48] This transition potentially leaves the rest of a corrupt organization intact. Obtaining evidence of corruption in an Office of Inspector General may be difficult, if not impossible, because the Office of Inspector General is the evidence gatherer.

The potential depth and complexity of allopoly formation in and between such oversight functions and the organizations they oversee cannot be overstated.

Promotions and lateral moves into and out of the overseer's organization and agreements to hire the family of a person in a different agency require mutually beneficial relationships. Adverse actions such as prosecution for violations of the law and at the other extreme, blackmail and extortion (coercion) will sour relations between the overseers and the organizations being overseen and can backfire.

A common allopoly for an overseer and a rule breaker to form (cooperation) is the overseer turning a blind eye to the rule breaker's actions, thus enabling them. Doing so can also create plausible deniability for the overseer. An overseer may also actively conceal rule breaking.

E.g.: Audits are a primary function of the Office of Inspector General. Constructive failures to adequately audit might include actions such as use of suspect data, insufficient, inadequate or unverified data; limiting the type or narrowing the scope of audits to deliberately avoid discovering violations; imposed limitations of inadequate tools and staff; elimination of competent staff; using time constraints to undermine an audit.

Offices of Inspectors General also have law enforcement departments. Arrests and convictions of non-government workers accused of fraud, waste and abuse of government programs are a visible output. These actions tend to not sour relations with government workers inside the agency that is overseen, as non-government workers are the target.

An Office of Inspector General might redirect its efforts from finding fraud, waste and abuse in government to the prosecution of citizens serviced by the overseen agency to produce visible results without antagonizing the agency it oversees.

This type of activity may be revealed by an increase in law enforcement actions against non-government workers and/or a reduction of actions against government agencies due to audits, along with scrutiny of the various means to do so surreptitiously.

These types of allopolistic activities may be revealed by the Office of Inspector General's assumption of the management or functions of the agency it oversees, as opposed to maintaining an oversight role.

Without substantive independent oversight, other issues will likely arise in the overseers' own organization.

E.g.: Such issues might be made visible by comparing the number of internal complaints, grievances, lawsuits (won/lost), settlements, settlements with non-disclosure agreements, etc., for the size of an Office of Inspector General, versus the same counts for larger government agencies.

Corrupt management of any oversight organization would logically fear and take concerted action against employees who may reveal the corruption. This is a form of concealment.

E.g.: Corrupt management and collusion in an Office of Inspector General may be made visible by scrutiny of employment records of employees who performed well and, without any evidence of physical or mental impairment, due to alleged uncharacteristic behavior become the subjects of adverse personnel actions that force the employees out.

A corrupt government oversight organization can cloak corruption in patriotism.

E.g.: Law enforcement organizations request warrants issued by the judicial branch of government to obtain records about specific individuals under investigation. An Office of Inspector General has both an audit department and a law enforcement department.

By restructuring itself to circumvent privacy laws, such as the Privacy Act[49], an Office of Inspector General can have its law enforcement department collect entire databases containing data on millions of people from the organizations it oversees, under the guise of an audit, bypassing the judicial branch and the requirement to obtain a search warrant for an individual's information.

Having obtained so much information about individuals, the law enforcement department might then go "fishing", share data with other law enforcement agencies, perform parallel construction[50] and create data query "research" systems that include illegally obtained information to steer supposedly independent investigators using it toward specific individuals, or conceal exculpatory evidence by exclusion. This potential laundering of illegally obtained evidence can be concealed by subsequently finding other data correlated with the illegally obtained evidence and claiming that the other data were used. This type of activity might be characterized by statements like "the computer came up with it" or "it was in the search results".

If such activity is occurring, then it necessarily involves the complicity of multiple levels of management and legal staff. It may be difficult to identify this type of activity due to the secrecy of the Office of Inspector General that is combined with the secrecy of a law enforcement department.

Such activity might be made visible by reviewing the employment records of employees for adverse personnel actions that followed the employee's recognition of the potential illegality. Another indicator this activity is occurring may be law enforcement having staffing and infrastructure, or access to same, for machine learning or artificial intelligence, as such require large amounts of data that could not have reasonably been obtained via a warrant from the judicial branch for the investigation of a specific individual or business.

Unlike elected positions whose continued tenure is not certain, some government workers may be in place for 20 to 40 years. Thus, the extent of allopoly formation with and within an overseer's organization, between oversight organizations and the agencies overseen cannot be overestimated.

E.g.: If a different government department conducts an employee opinion survey in an Office of Inspector General, and if that different government organization also has an Office of Inspector General, then a low response rate may be an indication of collusion between independent Offices of Inspectors General. The Offices of Inspectors General need not communicate with each other to collude, as each knows the results of not acting in unison.

The progression of allopoly formation for an overseer's organization is similar to that of the government organization it oversees. Eventually, the focus of the individuals within the overseer's organization becomes that of self-interest at the expense of the government function they are supposed to perform. What follows is the corruption of the organization being overseen. The difference is that the overseer organization's implementation of *COROLLARY #1: Allopoly Secrecy, Cooperation, Coercion, and Force* gives the overseer's organization the same protection from the organization it oversees and even its own employees that a government has from its citizens.

The Cycle of Civilization (with Time as a Metric)

Using time as a metric gives a different perspective, for it does not matter how governments, a set of allopolies or a single allopoly contrive to impose allopolistic loss upon others. What matters is the accumulation of allopolistic loss.

The allopolistic loss imposed upon a population will increase to the point that the population will not or cannot tolerate it. Alternatively, the imposed loss may debilitate the country so greatly that it cannot protect or defend itself.

The cycle of civilization becomes visible because allopolistic loss is imposed in many forms but ultimately affects the individual's time.

The Rise of a Civilization

Keep in mind that the time scale of civilizations is hundreds of years. If a civilization is rising, the benefits in terms of the population's time, from government, economies of scale and technological development exceed the accumulation of allopolistic loss. The outlook of investment into infrastructure is longer. Use of permanent workers increases. The civilization grows. As the civilization grows, the education level increases. The civilization's technological development is a function of the level of education and number of people educated. Opportunities for the individual increase. The rise of a middle class is likely. It is a time of prosperity in which the majority of each generation fares better than the last.

The Decline of a Civilization

During the decline of a civilization, the accumulation of allopolistic loss in terms of the population's time exceeds the benefits of government, returns to scale of economy, and the offset of allopolistic loss from technological advancement.

The speed of the decline is a function of the concentration of allopolistic loss on the things for which the population has a low demand elasticity, such as infrastructure, water, energy, food, shelter, communication and transportation.

The outlook for investments in infrastructure shortens. Use of part-time workers increases. As allopoly formation with and within government progresses, the distinction between government and private enterprise blurs.

During this time, technological advancement will reach its peak. Technology developed for use against people, such as military weapons and training, will be increasingly used as a means of controlling the population. The level of education declines. Corruption will increase along with dishonesty and collusion. The majority of each generation will not fare as well as the previous generation.

Time vs. Currency

Time can be converted to money, and the converse is also true. Money can buy actual time in the form of hired help, and accumulated time in the form of objects and education.

However, currency systems are subject to fluctuations in value. Currency-based price indexes, such as real income, can be manipulated.[51]

Conversely, time-based price indexes that measure the amount of time an individual must work to purchase items are an inherently more accurate basis for comparing changes in costs over time. They are also a good measure of imposed allopolistic loss that affects the individual because they are not affected by the type of imposed loss, be it increased taxes, inflation, etc.

E.g.: This year, it took a person two hours of work to buy a loaf of bread. Five years ago, it took the same person with the same income one half-hour of work to buy that same loaf of bread. It does not matter whether the reason is increased taxes, imposed costs further up the supply chain or inflation. The measure of time shows the effect on the individual, regardless of the propaganda surrounding the reasons.

The imposition of allopolistic loss is generally a reduction in people's ability to maintain their quality of life for the same number of hours worked. Those at lower levels of an allopoly will suffer the greatest loss.

As a civilization rises it can be said that real income is increasing. However, it is more accurate to say that on a wide-scale individuals have the opportunity to increase their quality of life for the number of work hours.

A civilization starts declining as the accumulation of allopolistic loss exceeds the returns to scale of government and the allopolistic loss offsets from technological advances. While it may be said that real income begins decreasing, it is more accurate to say that on an increasingly wide scale, the individual cannot maintain the same quality of life for the same amount of time previously worked. The zenith of the civilization can be a series of peaks as technological advances, and, of course, politics and war may offset the accumulation of allopolistic loss for short periods.

Population Density, Mobility and Resources

The factors described in *COROLLARY #1: Allopoly Secrecy, Cooperation, Coercion, and Force* determine the degree to which allopolistic loss can be imposed or resisted. However, the ability of an allopoly to avoid the imposition of allopolistic loss is a function of population density as well as resources such as water, land and the level and type of technology that affect these factors.

When the population density is low and the available resources plentiful, an imposed-upon allopoly could move into unoccupied land, out of reach of the imposing allopoly (mobility). At the other extreme, when the population density is high, and the available resources are controlled, all the land is owned, and even obtaining water to survive has a significant cost, the imposition of allopolistic loss cannot be avoided.

In-between these extremes are efforts to keep the target allopoly from avoiding the imposition of allopolistic loss. Reducing mobility is one means to do so for, once corralled, individuals may be identified and allopolistic loss imposed.

COROLLARY #13: Reduction of Target Allopoly Mobility

Allopolies will attempt to control the mobility of the targets of allopolistic loss to reduce their ability to evade the imposition, reduce their anonymity and their ability to communicate.

Without an impediment to the imposition of allopolistic loss, increasing population density and increasingly limited resources result in an increasing rate of imposition of allopolistic loss on the culture.

Allopolistic Characteristics of Slavery

As we noted at the outset, the definition of slavery becomes clearer when it is blatant, but not otherwise.

E.g.: An employer of a free person says "Do this or I hire another", while the slave owner says "do this or starve", and the slave has no recourse.

Identification of allopolistic characteristics applicable to slavery might help define the term:

- Certainly, ***COROLLARY #1: Allopoly Secrecy, Cooperation, Coercion, and Force*** is applicable as force and coercion must exceed the ability of the enslaved to resist.

- Also applicable is ***COROLLARY #2: Reduction of Target Allopoly Secrecy*** otherwise the enslaved would be able to hide their means of revolt.

- ***COROLLARY #3: Increasing Control of Communication*** is applicable for preventing the enslaved from creating their own allopolies and organizing to free themselves.

- The enslaved cannot be permitted to be anonymous per ***COROLLARY #4: Reduction of Anonymity***.

- Nor can the enslaved be permitted to learn how to free themselves, per ***COROLLARY #5: Reduction of Education Level.***

- The enslaved cannot be permitted to flee out of reach of those that would enslave them per ***COROLLARY #13: Reduction of Target Allopoly Mobility.***

These characteristics identify two differences between slaves and free persons.

The first difference is the manner and degree allopolistic elements are imposed. The second difference is the manner and degree allopolistic impositions can be resisted or avoided.

Whether the allopolistic loss is imposed by direct force or by the creation of law and circumstances that leave the individual no choice but to behave as a slave should not matter to the definition.

THE SLAVERY TAX RATE

The loss of the ability to create allopolies, or resist the imposition of allopolistic loss are characteristics of slavery, but they do not define it.

So, what is slavery?

In the mining example, putting an individual in a cage by force also takes the individual's time. So, too, does forcing an individual to work and then taking the benefits of that work by force. Most people would define this as slavery. In contrast, in the robber example, the couple's time was taken but the couple is not considered slaves.

The difference between the two examples is that in the mining case, the taking of the miners' time occurred during its use over a period of time. In the robber case, the taking of the couple's time occurred in a brief moment, after the couple's time had been accumulated in their possessions over a much longer time.

We postponed a review of historical studies of slavery until we better understood the nature of our inability to describe slavery in objective terms. We now understand slavery to be a type of allopoly. Like descriptions of governments, descriptions of slavery are made at a point in time.[52][53] This is not surprising because if slavery is generally practiced, it is supported by the government.

We can abstract slavery into two categories of allopolistic control: First, the enslaved as property, and second, the time of the enslaved as property or commodity, depending on circumstances. These categories are illustrated in the following two scenarios.

Slavery Scenario 1

The enslaved are property. There is an infinite number of variations in the conditions of the enslaved regarding the amount of self-determination and their social standing. However, there are two primary aspects with respect to allopoly theory.

First is the economic aspect. The slave's abilities, skills and education are determinants of the slave's productivity, as is the slave owner's ability to manage their workforce. If the cost of the enslaved, including their maintenance, is less than that of contracting a free person to do the work, then slavery remains a viable practice. What is taken from the enslaved is their time, privacy and their ability to resist the imposition of allopolistic loss in any form.

Second is the social aspect. A prominent feature of an individual being property is their isolation from society, that is, the imposed limits on the slave's ability to communicate, join and create allopolies and other forms of self-determination.

The slave must eat, sleep and live after the work day equivalent. The slave's time after work is also taken and the slave has no recourse. In other words, 100% of the slave's time is taken. It is likely that the slave's work-day equivalent produces the most value because it is after the work day that the majority of costs are incurred, such as food and shelter.

Children born to slaves can be the owner's property, and although the investment profit is not realized for many years, it may also include indoctrination of the enslaved. Depending on circumstances, the imposed dependence upon the slave owner may also foster loyalty, and so on.

<u>Slavery Scenario 2</u>

Manipulation of law and economic conditions to create an oversupply of workers. High unemployment forces workers to accept the low-to-subsistence-level wages offered or starve.

However, high unemployment can lead to social unrest and crime. The cost of controlling crime, protests, strikes and rebellion may be reduced by a militarized police force if a population can be disarmed per *COROLLARY #1: Allopoly Secrecy, Cooperation, Coercion, and Force*, its secrecy can be reduced per *COROLLARY #2: Reduction of Target Allopoly Secrecy*, its communication can be controlled per *COROLLARY #3: Increasing Control of Communication*, its anonymity can be eliminated per *COROLLARY #4: Reduction of Anonymity*, its ability to understand what is occurring can be reduced per *COROLLARY #5: Reduction of Education Level* and its mobility can be limited per *COROLLARY #13: Reduction of Target Allopoly Mobility*. That is, the application of the allopolistic characteristics we associate with slavery.

In the first scenario the slave owner must pay to purchase, maintain the slaves and enforce the slavery but does not negotiate a wage. In the second scenario, the employer pays a low wage via the unemployed who have no choice but to underbid each other. The employer does not invest in the purchase or maintenance of slaves, nor pays directly in the enforcement of slavery as the enslaved also pay taxes for their own enslavement.

What these two scenarios have in common is that the desired commodity is the worker's time at a price that the slave owner or employer is willing to pay, but the worker would not accept, given a choice.

The differences are how the worker's time is exacted or how the allopolistic loss is imposed.

Could the metric of an individual's time be used to define slavery?

The Slavery Tax Rate of Government Workers (STR$_w$)

In the mining example, the government was created at the point where benefits accrued to all involved. That government also had a cost: the time the miners would expend to pay for the police to protect them from bandits.

One can assume that each person spends their time enhancing their own quality of life. One can further assume that there is an average amount of time that each person in a population spends in doing so. Using the standard United States work week as an example, such a time expenditure may be estimated at 8 hours per day, 40 hours per week and 2,000 hours per year.

Thus, the total time spent improving of the quality of life of the entire population is the number of individuals multiplied by the average time each individual spends improving their quality of life.

Because they are part of the population, each government worker also spends their time improving their quality of life. Because this time is spent serving the government, the population must spend their time to pay for it. The cost of the government worker becomes the tax a government imposes on the population, including the government workers themselves.

The total cost of government workers is the number of government workers multiplied by the average amount of time the population must spend to pay the government workers.

The metric can be used for both government workers and non-government workers because it is an average of the population's work time. The calculation follows:

$P \ =$ The number of working individuals in the population.

$G \ =$ The number of government workers in the population (P).

$\overline{T} \ =$ The average time an individual in the population (P) spends working.

$P \cdot \overline{T} \ =$ The total time spent by the population (P) working to improve their quality of life, including government workers (G).

$G \cdot \overline{T} \ =$ The total time spent by the population (P) to pay for government workers (G).

The ratio of total time spent paying for government workers, to the total time spent working is the defacto tax rate in average time. An evenly distributed* tax that pays for government workers then becomes:

$$\text{Tax} \ = \ \frac{G \cdot \overline{T}}{P \cdot \overline{T}} \ = \ \frac{G}{P} \ \% \ \text{ of work time (hours)}$$

*Note: The government worker also derives benefit from the government and also pays the tax.

Now we have a theory to test.

If there were a population of ten and one person worked in government, each member of the population would spend $1/10^{th}$ of their time as a tax to pay for the one person in government as follows:

If $P = 10$ and $G = 1$, then

$$\text{Tax} = \frac{G}{P} = \frac{1}{10} = 10\% \text{ of each person's time.}$$

If the tax collected by the government (the one worker) were greater than 10% of each person's time, would the non-government workers be slaves?

At the extreme, if half the population were in the government, then the population would have to spend 50% of their time to pay for those in government.

If $G = \dfrac{P}{2}$, then

$$\text{Tax} = \frac{G}{P} = \frac{\left(\dfrac{P}{2}\right)}{P} = \frac{1}{2} = 50\% \text{ of each person's time.}$$

If the tax collected by the government workers, from the non-government workers were greater than 50% of their time, then would the non-government workers be slaves?

If there were a number N of the population P who were able to control the government so that they did not pay taxes, would forcing the population that was not in N, that being $P-N$, to pay N's taxes, make them $(P-N)$ slaves?

This calculation could determine the point of enslavement if the answer to the preceding three questions could be "yes". That is, the slavery tax rate due to the cost of government workers, denoted STR_W, is:

$$STR_W = \frac{G}{P} \% \text{ of } \overline{T} \text{ hours of the individual's time.}$$

Using the inverse of the slavery tax rate of government workers gives a direct and objective measure of the number of population members per government worker, that is, $\frac{1}{STR_W} = \frac{P}{G}$, as shown in Table 1.

Table 1: *Slavery Tax Rate shown as Population to Government Worker ratio* $\left(\frac{P}{G}\right)$

$\frac{P}{G}$	$STR_W = \frac{G}{P}\%$	$\frac{P}{G}$	$STR_W = \frac{G}{P}\%$
1	100 %	15	7 %
2	50 %	20	5 %
3	33 %	25	4 %
4	25 %	50	2 %
5	20 %	100	1 %
6	17 %	200	0.50 %
7	14 %	300	0.33 %
8	13 %	400	0.25 %
9	11 %	500	0.20 %
10	10 %	1,000	0.10 %

A plot of the Slavery Tax Rate is informative, as shown in Figure 2.

Figure 2: Slavery Tax Rate (STRw) as Percent of the Individual's Time vs Total Imposed Tax vs P/G Ratio

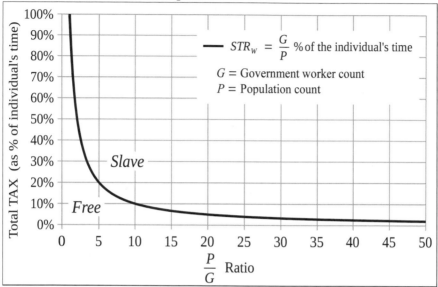

Interpretation of the Slavery Tax Rate for Government Workers

A government provides desired services when the fully informed population consents to be taxed. The total taxes and costs imposed (TAX) upon an individual, in terms of the time of that individual, can only assume one of three relative values with respect to the slavery tax rate (STRw): Less than, equal to or greater than.

If TAX is less than the STRw then, if the population is content with the services it provides, the government returns more than it costs. This outcome occurs when the allopolistic loss imposed or permitted by government is smaller its returns to scale, technology offsets, etc.

If TAX is equal to the STRw then, if the population is content with the services it provides, government returns what it costs. This is the logical point beyond which a government imposes slavery.

If TAX is greater than the STR_W, then government costs more than it returns. Absent investment in future time reductions, the government is likely forcing individuals into slavery.

Absent allopolistic loss, an organized government can be more efficient in working toward common goals than non-government workers contributing a small percentage of their time in an unorganized manner. Furthermore, a government could be expected to make expenditures to reduce its costs and thereby reduce the tax it imposes.

E.g.: A government purchases a truck and a snowplow attachment. A single truck with a snowplow can plow the snow from both lanes of 50 miles of road in much less time, and at less cost, than 100 people with shovels. That truck can also be used for other things, which further reduces the cost of government. Hence, the government need not employ 100 people and instead purchases the truck and the plow.

However, the savings would not be as great if the government paid ten times more for the truck than anyone else would have paid. Such would be the case if an allopoly were created in the form of a kick-back scheme between the people in the government who made the purchase decision and the company that sold the truck. In this case, the taxes required to pay for government would increase with respect to the slavery tax rate, by the amount of the overpayment.

At the other extreme, government workers could decide to use the government's allopoly on coercive force over the population to improve their own quality of life.

E.g.: Government officials decide that their time is worth ten times that of a citizen. The taxes collected by the government would increase with respect to its slavery tax rate.

Generally, as a population increases, so does the size of its government. The government could realize increasing returns to scale. However, *THEOREM #1: The Driving Force of Allopoly Creation* and *THEOREM #3: Preference to Form Allopolies with Governing Allopolies* predict that allopolies would be formed in and with government. Allopolistic losses would increase taxes with respect to the slavery tax rate.

THEOREM #14: The Slavery Tax Rate due to Government Workers.

The slavery tax rate due to government workers, that is, labor, is the rate at which a government returns as much as it takes from the population in terms of individual time.

The slavery tax rate due to government workers, is denoted as STR_W and is shown in Equation 1.

Equation 1

$$STR_W = \frac{G}{P} \text{ \% of the individual's standard work time.}$$

Where:

P = The number of people in the population that work and pay taxes, both government and non-government.

G = The number of people in the population that work for government.

Government Workers

The allopolistic structure of government in the United States, that is, the structure by which taxes are collected from the population has federal, state, county, and municipal levels. For the example computations in this text, levels below state government will be categorized as local government.

Federal Government Workers

The federal government collects taxes from the population under its control, which is all the citizens in all the states, and other territories controlled by the United States. The federal government employs federal government workers, denoted as G_F.

State Government Workers

State governments are semi-sovereign. State governments may collect taxes from the population under their control. States control counties, municipalities and territory within their boundaries that are not controlled by the federal government. The states employ state government workers, denoted as G_S.

County Government Workers

County governments collect taxes from the population under their control. Counties contain both municipalities, and territory not controlled directly by municipalities, the state or the federal government. Counties may be known by other names such as parishes, townships or boroughs. Counties employ county government workers, denoted as G_C.

Some state-level entities such as Washington, D.C., do not have county governments. At least one state, Connecticut, abolished its county governments.[54]

Municipal Government Workers

Municipal governments collect taxes from the population under their control. Municipalities (cities, towns, townships, etc.) employ municipal government workers, denoted as G_M.

The total number of government workers, denoted (G) is counted for all government hierarchies in Equation 2.

Equation 2

$$G = G_F + \sum_{i=1}^{\substack{\text{Number of} \\ \text{States}}} \sum_{j=1}^{\substack{\text{Number of} \\ \text{Counties}}} \sum_{k=1}^{\substack{\text{Number of} \\ \text{Municipalities}}} \left(G_{S_i} + G_{C_{i,j}} + G_{M_{i,j,k}} \right)$$

A computational method for the tally of government workers from a lower level in the hierarchy to the higher (right to left) is shown in Equation 3

Equation 3

$$G = G_F + \sum_{i=1}^{\substack{\text{Number of} \\ \text{States}}} G_{S_i} + \sum_{j=1}^{\substack{\text{Number of} \\ \text{Counties}}} G_{C_{i,j}} + \sum_{k=1}^{\substack{\text{Number of} \\ \text{Municipalities}}} G_{M_{i,j,k}}$$

Population

For counting purposes, populations are geographically bound at a point in time. Unlike government worker counts that can be tallied by the hiring government body, the territorial coverage of states, counties and municipalities overlap. The population of a state (P_S) includes the population of all the counties (P_C) within the state. The population of a county generally includes the populations of the different municipalities (P_M) located within them.

Computation of the Slavery Tax Rate of Government Worker Costs

The slavery tax rate of any particular government hierarchy level is the number of government workers divided by the population over which the government has domain. This ratio has the benefit of being a "government worker per population member" ratio that needs only to be multiplied by the number of people in the relevant population to obtain the number of associated government workers.

$$\text{Federal government workers per person} = \frac{G_F}{P}$$

$$\text{State government workers per person} = \frac{G_S}{P_S}$$

$$\text{County government workers per person} = \frac{G_C}{P_C}$$

$$\text{Municipality government workers per person} = \frac{G_M}{P_M}$$

The estimate of the total number of government workers working for the population of a particular government hierarchy, for example, a municipality, is equal to the municipality population multiplied by the sum of each type of government-worker-per-population-member ratio, from highest to lowest, effective in the municipality. This calculation is shown in Equation 4:

Equation 4

$$\sum_M G = \left(\frac{G_F}{P} + \frac{G_S}{P_S} + \frac{G_C}{P_C} + \frac{G_M}{P_M} \right) P_M$$

Dividing both sides of Equation 4 by the municipality population (P_M), as shown in Equation 5, yields the simplification that the slavery tax rate can be computed by simply adding the relevant $\frac{G}{P}$ ratios of higher levels of government and populations to the lower ones.

Equation 5

$$STR_{W_M} = \frac{\sum\limits_M G}{P_M} = \frac{G_F}{P} + \frac{G_S}{P_S} + \frac{G_C}{P_C} + \frac{G_M}{P_M}$$

Number of United States Government Hierarchies

In 2017, the United States had its federal government, 50 state governments, 3,031 county governments and 35,748 sub-county governments.[55]

The Slavery Tax Rate for Non-Labor Costs (STR$_N$) and Specific Amounts

The population is taxed the same amount of work time for non-labor costs and specific amounts, with the exception of individuals at the poverty level of income.

Calculation of the Slavery Tax Rate for Government Non-Labor Costs and Specific Amounts

The total amount each individual earns in a year is divided by the total number of hours the individual worked that year, yielding an annual hourly rate, as shown in Equation 6.

Equation 6

$$w_i = \frac{y_i}{t_i}$$

Where:
y_i = Individual total annual income.
t_i = Individual total annual work hours.
w_i = Individual annual hourly income.

The individual annual hourly incomes (w_i) for the relevant population are summed to give a total annual hourly income denoted by W_P, as shown in Equation 7.

Equation 7

$$W_P = \sum_{i=1}^{\substack{\text{Relevant} \\ \text{Population (P)}}} w_i$$

The total non-labor cost for a particular population is denoted by C_P. Every individual will contribute the same amount of work time, denoted by s_i, to pay for the non-labor cost. The non-labor cost (C_P) is divided by the population's total annual hourly income (W_P), as shown in Equation 8.

Equation 8

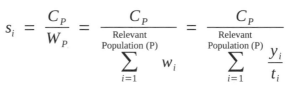

$$s_i = \frac{C_P}{W_P} = \frac{C_P}{\sum_{i=1}^{\substack{\text{Relevant} \\ \text{Population (P)}}} w_i} = \frac{C_P}{\sum_{i=1}^{\substack{\text{Relevant} \\ \text{Population (P)}}} \frac{y_i}{t_i}}$$

The slavery tax rate for a non-labor cost, denoted by c_P is computed by dividing the number of hours each member of the population will work, by the number of standard work hours in the year, denoted by S_Y, as shown in Equation 9. For the examples in this text, we assume there are 50 weeks in a year, and the standard work time is 40 hours per week, yielding a standard work time of 2,000 hours for a standard work year.

Equation 9

$$c_p = \frac{s_i}{S_Y}$$

E.g.: A population (P) has ten people, each with a specific income earned in a year, as shown in Table 2. The total government facility non-labor maintenance cost (C_P) is $1,000. The entire population, excluding those at the poverty level, had a combined annual hourly income of $392.07 per hour.

Table 2: Illustration of the slavery tax rate (c_P) computation for non-labor costs (C_P) of \$1,000, for a population of ten people, with a standard work year (S_Y) of 2,000 hours.

Person (i)	Total Work Year Income y_i (\$/year)	Average Work Hours (hrs/wk)	Total Hours Worked Per Year t_i (hrs/year)	Annual Hourly Income w_i (\$/hr)	Equal Work Time			Percent of Total Income		
					Work Hours to Pay for non-Labor Tax s_i (hrs)	Dollars paid for non-Labor Tax (\$)	Work Hours as Percent of Standard Work Year c_P (%)	Percent of Total Income to Pay for non-Labor Tax (%)	Work Hours to Pay for non-Labor Tax (hrs)	Dollars Paid for non-Labor Cost (\$)
1	\$165,902	20	1,000	\$165.90	2.6	\$423	0.13%	0.15%	1.5	\$247
2	\$78,041	40	2,000	\$39.02	2.6	\$100	0.13%	0.15%	3.0	\$116
3	\$77,609	40	2,000	\$38.80	2.6	\$99	0.13%	0.15%	3.0	\$116
4	\$74,687	40	2,000	\$37.34	2.6	\$95	0.13%	0.15%	3.0	\$111
5	\$70,565	80	4,000	\$17.64	2.6	\$45	0.13%	0.15%	6.0	\$105
6	\$55,236	60	3,000	\$18.41	2.6	\$47	0.13%	0.15%	4.5	\$82
7	\$53,941	40	2,000	\$26.97	2.6	\$69	0.13%	0.15%	3.0	\$80
8	\$48,737	40	2,000	\$24.37	2.6	\$62	0.13%	0.15%	3.0	\$73
9	\$47,215	40	2,000	\$23.61	2.6	\$60	0.13%	0.15%	3.0	\$70
10	\$10,875*	30	1,500	\$7.25*	0.0	\$0	0.00%	0.00%	0.0	\$0
Y_P =	\$671,933			W_P = \$392.07		\$1,000				\$1,000

*Excluded from calculation. In this example individuals below the poverty level are not taxed.

A currency-based tax generally conceals the different amounts of work time taken to pay the tax.

The work hours for each member of the population required to pay for the non-Labor cost are calculated by inserting the values from Table 2 into Equation 8:

$$s_i = \frac{C_p}{W_P} = \frac{\$1,000}{392.07\,\dfrac{\$}{\text{hour}}} = 2.6 \text{ hours}$$

The slavery tax rate is computed by dividing the work hours (s_i) by the standard annual work time (S_Y), using Equation 9:

$$c_P = \frac{s_i}{S_Y} = \frac{2.6 \text{ hours}}{2,000 \text{ hours}} = 0.13\%$$

While each individual spends the same amount of work time to pay the tax, the amount of money each pays varies based upon what each earns in that amount of time, as shown in Table 2.

Inherent Fairness of the Slavery Tax Rate Calculation

The slavery tax rate is a time-based metric. A currency-based tax, such as a percent of total income, conceals the fact that it makes some people work more hours than others to pay for the same tax. It does this by presuming that all people work the same amount of time. This would be the case only if all the individual annual work times (t_i) in Equation 8 were the same.

It is not realistic to presume equal annual work hours for a work force of mixed full-time labor and part-time labor and associated euphemisms such as "the gig economy".

Because the taking of an individual's time is the defining characteristic of slavery, taking an individual's time to give to another is not a minor point. This is shown in the "Percent of Total Income" column of Table 2.

Summing the Slavery Tax Rate for Labor, Non-Labor Government, and specific Costs.

The slavery tax rate of non-labor costs, denoted as STR_N, for a population is the sum for each government level that imposes the taxes, as shown in Equation 10:

Equation 10

$$STR_N = \sum_F c_F + \sum_S c_S + \sum_C c_C + \sum_M c_M$$

Because it is a percentage of the individual's standard time, the slavery tax rate for non-labor government costs (STR_N) can be added directly to the slavery tax rate for government workers (STR_W) in Equation 5 to obtain the slavery tax rate (STR), as shown in Equation 11. This same calculation can be made for all non-labor costs, at all government levels.

Equation 11

$$STR = STR_W + STR_N$$

$$= \frac{G_F}{P} + \frac{G_S}{P_S} + \frac{G_C}{P_C} + \frac{G_M}{P_M}$$

$$+ \sum_F c_F + \sum_S c_S + \sum_C c_C + \sum_M c_M$$

Where:

$\sum_F c_F$ = Federal non-labor Slavery Tax Rates

$\sum_S c_S$ = State non-labor Slavery Tax Rates

$\sum_C c_C$ = County non-labor Slavery Tax Rates

$\sum_M c_M$ = Municipal non-labor Slavery Tax Rates

Government Interest Payments

Government interest payments are a type of non-labor costs for which the slavery tax rate is calculated in the same manner. However, the slavery tax rate computation for interest payments has some useful interpretations and features for government policy makers, government planners and citizens alike as shown in the following example:

E.g.: From 2001 through 2005, each year it took the entire working population of a state 0.12% of its time to pay for the materials and loan interest to maintain its capitol building. The interest payments took 0.02% of the population's time each year. At the end of 2005, the loan was paid off. Thus, it took 0.02% of each individual's standard work time each year, for five years to pay for the interest. Because the work time to pay for the interest is calculated in the year incurred, it can be summed without adjustment:

$$0.02\% \times 2,000 \frac{\text{hours}}{\text{year}} \times 5 \text{ years} = 2 \text{ hours}$$

Note: The use of the slavery tax rate computation in this manner does not require a lookup of the population or government worker counts.

Two misconceptions are easy to make with respect to the computation of the slavery tax rate for non-labor costs.

First, the slavery tax rate is not based upon annual income. Each individual in the population is taxed based upon the same amount of standard work time. See *QUESTION #1: How does the Slavery Tax Rate differ from a flat tax?* for more detail.

Second, that expenditures that typically come with labor costs may include labor. No, they may not.

E.g.: A building may be leased, but the costs of any labor that accompanies the lease, such as groundskeepers, janitors, engineers, electricians, etc., should not be included in the non-labor costs. Instead, the labor costs should be added to the tally of labor costs as government employees. Otherwise the actual number of government workers would be concealed. See **QUESTION #4: Should only full-time government workers be counted in (G)?** for more detail.

As the computation of the slavery tax rate for non-labor government costs contributes little in the way of additional knowledge, it will be omitted for most of the remainder of this text.

Government Transfer Payments

Transfer payments between different government hierarchies will not affect the computation of the total slavery tax rate, as it is a reference by which to compare the combined imposed taxes by all government hierarchies.

However, government transfer payments will affect the comparison of taxes collected by different levels of government to their respective slavery tax rates. Thus the slavery tax rate is a visible measure of a higher level government's usurpation of power from lower government levels through the use of taxes.

E.g.: The federal government increases personal income taxes in excess of its slavery tax rate and then exerts control over state governments by offering money. The state governments, limited by the amount the federal government has already taxed its citizens, cannot raise taxes any higher without angering the public. The states may or may not alter the number of state government workers, etc. The total slavery tax rate computation is cumulative and is therefore unaffected by the transfer. The comparison of the individual's total taxes to the total slavery tax rate will not change.

However, the individual may find that the taxes imposed by the federal government exceed the federal government's slavery tax rate $\left(\dfrac{G_F}{P} + \sum\limits_F c_F\right)$. At the same time, that same individual may find that the taxes imposed by the state government are less than the state's slavery tax rate $\left(\dfrac{G_S}{P_S} + \sum\limits_S c_S\right)$, and so on.

Regressive Taxes

A regressive tax negatively affects lower-income individuals disproportionately to those with higher incomes. A flat tax on income is one example of a regressive tax.

E.g.: Assume a flat tax of 10% on income. A person that makes $100,000 per year would be less negatively affected when taxed $10,000, than the person who makes $1,000 per year and is taxed $100.

In the example shown in Table 2 individual #10 has an income below the poverty level. Generally, individuals making near or less than the poverty level should not be taxed. If low-income individuals are not taxed, the slavery tax rate for non-labor expenses would then be recalculated for the remaining nine individuals, as is also shown in Table 2. Alternatively, the low-income individuals could be taxed, but then given financial aid by the government. Either method results in an increase in the slavery tax rate for the tax payers. For more details, see **QUESTION #4: Should only full-time government workers be counted in (G)?**

Business Taxes

Business entities are allopolies that function to make allopolistic gains for the people who own them. Businesses can operate in a single municipality or across multiple municipalities, counties and states. In doing so, business entities use the infrastructure paid for and maintained by the particular government hierarchies in which they operate to obtain their revenues. The taxes paid by a business entity should support the resources and infrastructure that allow it make it money according to its use, and non-use (control) if applicable. That is, the slavery tax rate for a business is its share of its use and control of infrastructure and resources.

The interpretation of the slavery tax rate for business is different than for individuals. A government that taxes a business more than its slavery tax rate is forcing the business to subsidize the government. A government that taxes a business less than its slavery tax rate is forcing the government's respective populations to subsidize the business, in which case the subsidy should be tallied as tax on the respective populations.

Businesses providing goods or services in government regulated industries or infrastructure with inelastic demand, that charge lower prices to its client businesses than to individuals, are effectively taxing the individuals in order to subsidize its client businesses. This situation is usually the result of allopolistic activity. The subsidy should be tallied as a tax on the individual.

Implementation

So that individuals can tally the total taxes they pay, businesses could be required to clearly mark the tax amount of the prices of the goods or services they provide. Similarly, government taxing bodies can collect the individual hours worked when it collects income data.

E.g.: A food product has a label displaying the ingredients and warnings. The manufacturer could be required to list the total sum of government-imposed costs on the product up to the point of shipping and provide the retailer with a list of additional taxes and costs imposed by the respective government hierarchies to the point of delivery. The retailer could post these amounts along with those at the point of sale so that purchasers could tally them.

The Slavery Tax Rate Using Real Data

United States government data for population[56][57], unemployment [58], federal[59][60] and state [61] government employee counts and income[62] are used. Data for Washington D.C. are shown in Table 3.

The computation of the slavery tax rate of non-labor costs (STR_N) is not included in most of these examples because it adds little in the way of knowledge.

The slavery tax rate is computed with respect to the individuals who pay it, not the entire population $(P_{[all]})$. People who do not pay taxes are removed from population estimates when calculating the slavery tax rate. For the examples in this text, children aged 17 years or less do not work. Adults aged 65+ years will be assumed to not pay taxes. This leaves the population ages 18-64 years $(P_{[18-64]})$ as the working population. The unemployed (P_U) come from the working population and are also subtracted from the relevant level of government when computing the slavery tax rate, shown in Equation 12:

Equation 12

$$P = P_{[18-64]} - P_U$$

This adjustment, shown in Table 3, has the effect of raising the slavery tax rate for those who pay for government. Examples later in this text will show how entitlements for these populations are handled.

Table 3: Slavery Tax Rate Data for Washington D.C., 2018

Government Hierarchy (Summation Level)	Government Workers (G)	Population ages 18-64 years less the unemployed. $\left(P_{[18-64]} - P_U\right)$	Slavery Tax Rate $\left(\dfrac{G}{P}\right)$
Federal (F)	(G_F) 5,469,064	(P) 193,725,422	2.82%
State (S)	(G_S) 42,200	(P_S) 458,013	9.21%
County*	-	-	-
Municipality*	-	-	-
*Washington D.C. has no counties or municipalities.			

Because Washington D.C. has no counties or municipalities[63], the county and municipality terms can be dropped from Equation 5 to compute the Slavery Tax Rate for the state (STR_W), as shown in Equation 13:

Equation 13

$$STR_W = \frac{\sum\limits_{S} G}{P_S} = \frac{G_F}{P} + \frac{G_S}{P_S}$$

Substituting the corresponding values from Table 3 into Equation 13 yields the Slavery Tax Rate for Washington D.C. in 2018, in terms of the individual's work time.

$$STR_W = 2.82\% + 9.21\% = 12.0\%$$

This is shown in Figure 3, along with the other states.

Although there can be significant differences in taxation between municipalities, for illustrative purposes, a shorthand is used for local government (L) within a state that combines counties and municipalities. The term G_{S+L} will denote the total number of state, county and municipal government workers in a state, as shown in Equation 14:

Equation 14

$$STR_W = \frac{\sum\limits_S G}{P_S} = \frac{G_F}{P} + \frac{G_{S+L}}{P_S}$$

The number of state and local government workers and the population of each state are variables. The Slavery Tax Rate is computed for each state in Figure 3.

Table 4 shows the government worker and population data for Wyoming and the slavery tax rate computations for the illustrative examples that follow here and in the Questions section.

Table 4: Slavery Tax Rate Data for Wyoming (WY), 2018

Government Hierarchy (Summation Level)	Government Workers (G)		Population ages 18-64 years less the unemployed. $(P_{[18-64]} - P_U)$	Slavery Tax Rate $\left(\dfrac{G}{P}\right)$
Federal (F)	(G_F)	5,469,064	(P) 193,725,422	2.82%
State + Local (S)	(G_{S+L})	61,200	(P_S) 344,988	17.74%
Unemployed (S)	(P_U)	11,352	--	--
Age 65+ (S)	(G_{65+})	87,777	(P_S) 344,988	25.44%

The slavery tax rate for the state of Wyoming (WY) in Figure 3 is computed by inserting the corresponding values from Table 4 into Equation 14:

$$STR_W = 2.82\% + 17.74\% = 20.6\%$$

Figure 3:   *2018 U.S. Slavery Tax Rate by State using the working age population 18 to 64 years. (excluding non-labor costs)*

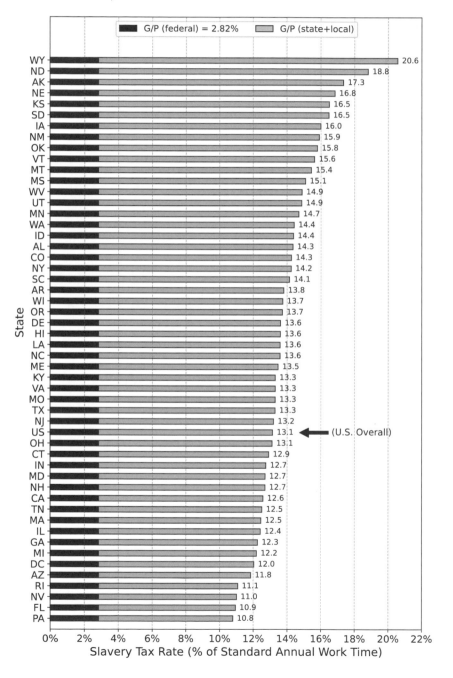

Based solely on the number of government workers, as shown in Figure 3, Wyoming (WY) at 20.6% of the population's time, has a higher slavery tax rate than Pennsylvania (PA), which is 10.8%.

The people of Wyoming will determine if they want the services provided by the larger state and local government worker-to-population ratio. The people might also decide to live with fewer services if they believe that the government is imposing the cost of an unwanted number of state and local employees. The slavery tax rate is a visible metric for this determination.

The answer to **QUESTION #7: How many government workers are required for each citizen?** uses Figure 6 to provide perspective on the various states' number of government workers and populations.

Note that the shorthand of state + local government used for demonstration combines all the county and municipal government workers to the state level. The actual slavery tax rate computations should be made for the population with its relevant government workers, as different counties and municipalities have different numbers of government workers and provide different services.

The implementation of the slavery tax rate calculation can be made relatively easy by each level of government as each must pay their workers, and each should have a count of their workers, the amounts paid and the hours worked. Each level of government must also pay for its non-labor costs and should be able to provide them. The costs of contractors providing services to the government can also be obtained because the government can impose reporting requirements, such as breaking down labor, hours worked and non-labor costs in a contract.

The slavery tax rate raises several questions. More detail is provided in the Questions section that follows.

QUESTIONS

A few obvious questions arise. Most are directly answerable using the slavery tax rate computation or the use of time as a measure.

QUESTION #1: How does the Slavery Tax Rate differ from a flat tax?

Although the slavery tax rate can be converted at any specific point in time to a currency based percentage of income tax, there are three primary differences.

First: The slavery tax rate is based on an individual's time. An individual's income, proportional to a standard work time, is what is taxed for example, 40 hours per week or 2,000 hours per year.

E.g: A slavery tax rate of 5% would be interpreted as 5% of 2,000 hours/year, that is 100 hours of their annual work time. A person that made $50/hr in a standard work year would be taxed $5,000.

Because the slavery tax rate is based upon the individual's time, it does not conceal allopolistic loss in terms of the time of the individual, as a currency-based tax does. Nor does it penalize hard work.

E.g.: A person worked two full-time jobs, that is 4,000 hours to make $30,000. That is $7.50 per hour. A standard work year of 2,000 hours means a slavery tax rate of 5% is 100 hours. For this person that means a tax of $750. An income-based tax system conceals the imposition of allopolistic loss by taxing the total income of $30,000 at 5%, or $1,500. Thus the imposition of allopolistic loss becomes both visible, and measurable.

Second: The slavery tax rate is visible and directly related to the work government is supposed to perform, based upon the number of people in government service, for any government hierarchy: federal, state and local.

E.g.: A 10% Slavery Tax Rate means that one-in-ten members of the population are full-time government workers. At a slavery tax rate of 10%, out of a village of 100 people, 90 people would be non-government workers, and 10 people would be full-time government workers.

Third: The slavery tax rate can be used to track the allopolistic loss or dysfunction of government. Comparisons of the mean and median incomes between government and non-government workers, and other robust statistical methods for comparing income distributions may be used to determine the degree to which the government worker income distribution varies from non-government workers. The results of this comparison, combined with the comparison of the slavery tax rate to the actual taxes collected, will yield an indicator of the degree of government dysfunction and changes over time.

QUESTION #2: Should all taxes be counted against the slavery tax rate?

Yes. The classification or stratification of government type (federal, state, local, etc.), or the tax classification (sales, VAT, property, etc.) is irrelevant. All government-associated taxes, surcharges, fees, costs, etc., should be counted, regardless of where in any supply chain they are imposed.

QUESTION #3:   Should government-mandated purchases of products or services from either government or non-government entities be counted as a tax?

Yes. This is a tax that is collected by proxy, regardless of how it is contrived.

QUESTION #4:   Should only full-time government workers be counted in (G)?

No. All people who benefit from allopolies granted by government should be counted as government workers, even if not officially government employees.

E.g.: A government dismisses all the functions of government, contracting out all government work to private companies. The tax paid by the citizens for the function of government goes to the contractor's employees. Therefore, the contractor and its employees serve as government employees.

Absent allopolistic loss, a government can generally provide the functions required of it for less cost than a private or for-profit company, for the simple reason that there is no profit.

Allopolistic loss imposed by a government contractor reducing the quantity or quality of goods or services, or increasing the time spent by the population in dealing with the contractor, must also be included as a tax imposed by the government.

QUESTION #5:   Should all the population be counted in (P)?

When computing the slavery tax rate P should be limited to the people that work and pay the taxes. Some points should be called out.

Spouses and Significant Others

Although a spouse may not have a paid job, maintaining a household requires time. A non-working spouse's unpaid time enables the working spouse to spend more time in paid work.

Working spouses pay taxes as a percent of their time. Non-working spouses use the benefits provided by the government. The taxes the non-working spouses would have paid are paid by the working population. It is a form of diffuse acquisition and concentrated collection.

Children

Some cultures have prohibitions against child labor and legal requirements that parents support their children. For this text, the preceding is assumed, and children should not be counted. For this text, children are people aged less than 18 years.

Retirees

In many cultures, children have no obligation to support their parents. In some cultures a government benefit, paid out of taxes, is provided to older people. For this text, the retirement age is 65+ years. Analyses for different countries, or purposes may have different parameters. The answer to ***QUESTION #6: How does the Slavery Tax Rate apply to those unable to work who receive government benefits?*** provides more explanation.

Do not be too quick to disregard the rest of the population for other types of analyses. You, too, may reach the age of retirement.

Unemployment

Unemployment benefits in the United States are a combination of both state and federal government efforts. The number of unemployed for each state differs. Absent overpopulation, the failure to plan for a robust economy and the failure to provide an education system so that there is employment at wages that can provide a living is likely the result of government action or inaction in terms of long-term planning, which is itself usually the result of allopolistic activity.

Some political and social considerations are that the unemployed need the resources to seek employment, including retraining and financial support during periods of unemployment. That cost can be weighed against the cost of incarceration for those who commit crimes to support their families.

Because the unemployed do not pay taxes*, the relevant population used is the same as shown in Equation 12.

Note: Taxing a government benefit is the equivalent of reducing the benefit and can be tallied as such.

Any government benefits given to the unemployed would be tallied as a government expense that would be paid by the working population (P_s).

The slavery tax rate for a benefit can be computed for a fixed amount, as shown in the following unemployment example, or for a percent of the standard annual income, as is shown in the next example for retirement benefits.

Continuing the illustrative example for Wyoming, for this example the unemployment benefit amount is $450 per week for 26 weeks, that is $11,700 per year, per unemployed.

From Table 4, the number of unemployed in Wyoming is 11,352. Multiplying these quantities yields the total unemployment benefit cost, denoted by C_{P_U} :

$$C_{P_U} = \$11{,}700 \times 11{,}352 = \$132{,}818{,}400$$

The total hourly income $\left(W_P\right)$ is not available because we lack the amount of time worked per individual $\left(t_i\right)$.

With the currency-based tax caveats shown in Table 2, <u>for this demonstration only</u>, we will presume that the tax payers in Wyoming all work the standard work time $\left(S_Y\right)$.

Continuing the notation from Table 2, the total annual income for a population, denoted as Y_P, is the total of the incomes of the all the population members, as shown in Equation 15:

Equation 15

$$Y_P = \sum_{i=1}^{\substack{\text{Relevant} \\ \text{Population (P)}}} y_i$$

Setting $t_i = S_y$ in Equation 9 yields Equation 16:

Equation 16

$$c_P = \frac{C_P}{\sum\limits_{i=1}^{\substack{\text{Relevant} \\ \text{Population (P)}}} \dfrac{y_i}{S_Y}} \cdot \frac{1}{S_Y} = \frac{C_P}{\sum\limits_{i=1}^{\substack{\text{Relevant} \\ \text{Population (P)}}} y_i} = \frac{C_P}{Y_P}$$

The total individual income $\left(Y_P\right)$ of Wyoming for 2018 is $22,175,102,000, as shown in Appendix B. Inserting these values into Equation 16 yields the slavery tax rate for the specific amount of unemployment benefits.

$$c_{P_U} = \frac{C_{P_U}}{Y_P} = \frac{\$132,818,400}{\$22,175,102,000} = 0.60\%$$

Substituting the corresponding values into Equation 11 yields Equation 17.

Equation 17

$$STR_{W_s} = \frac{\sum\limits_{S+L} G}{P_S} + \sum\limits_{S} c_S = \frac{G_F}{P} + \frac{G_{S+L}}{P_S} + c_{P_U}$$

Inserting c_{P_U} and the corresponding values from Table 4 into Equation 17 yields the slavery tax rate for Wyoming's government workers and unemployment benefits.

$$STR_{W_s} = 2.82\% + 17.74\% + 0.60\% = 21.2\%$$

Figure 4 illustrates the addition of the slavery tax rate for the same fixed unemployment benefit for all states.

QUESTION #6:   How does the Slavery Tax Rate apply to those unable to work who receive government benefits?

The Elderly

The elderly who receive retirement benefits from the federal government can be tallied as federal government workers (G_{65+}) because the expense is paid by taxes.

For this example assume that those ages 65+ retire and receive a retirement benefit from the government at the rate of one-half of the standard work time.

The slavery tax rate computation is again straightforward, as shown in Equation 18:

Figure 4: 2018 U.S. Slavery Tax Rate by State for the working age
population ages 18-64 and a fixed unemployment
amount*. (excluding non-labor costs)
*An income based tax percentage is used for demonstration.

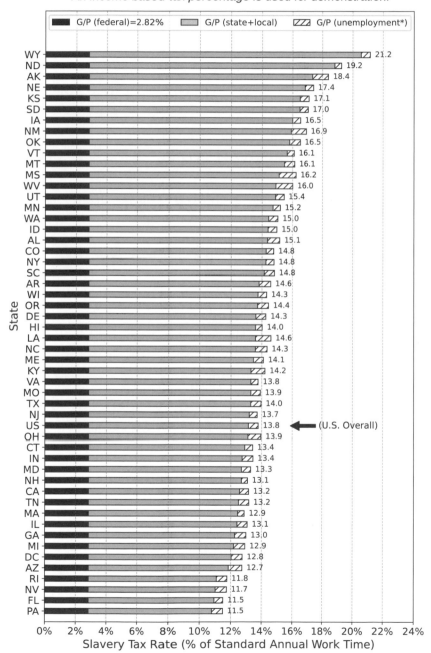

Equation 18

$$STR_{W_s} = \frac{G_F}{P} + \frac{G_{S+L}}{P_S} + c_{P_U} + \frac{G_{65+}}{P_S} \cdot \frac{1}{2}$$

Continuing the illustrative example, the slavery tax rate shown for Wyoming (WY) in Figure 5 is computed by inserting the corresponding values from Table 4 into Equation 18:

$$STR_{W_s} = 2.82\% + 17.74\% + 0.60\% + \frac{25.44}{2} = 33.9\%$$

Figure 5 shows the same calculation made for all the states.

Specific Interpretation of the Slavery Tax Rate

The interpretation of the slavery tax rate for Wyoming (WY), as shown in Figure 5, would be:

(a) If the people of Wyoming were informed and consented to the services government provided for the number of government workers; and

(b) if the people wanted to provide the unemployed benefits at the rate $450/wk for 26 weeks/year per person; and

(c) if the people wanted to provide retirement benefits for those aged 65+ years at the rate of half the standard work time; then the working population $\left(P_{[18-64]} - P_U\right)$ of Wyoming would not be forced into slavery until the total taxes and costs imposed upon each exceeded what they each earned in 33.9% of the standard annual work time, that is:

$$0.339 \times 2{,}000 \text{ hours} = 678 \text{ hours} = 17 \text{ weeks}$$

Figure 5: 2018 U.S. Slavery Tax Rate by State for the working age population ages 18-64, fixed unemployment amount* and retired ages 65+ with benefits at half the rate of standard work time. (excluding non-labor costs)
An income based tax percentage is used for demonstration.

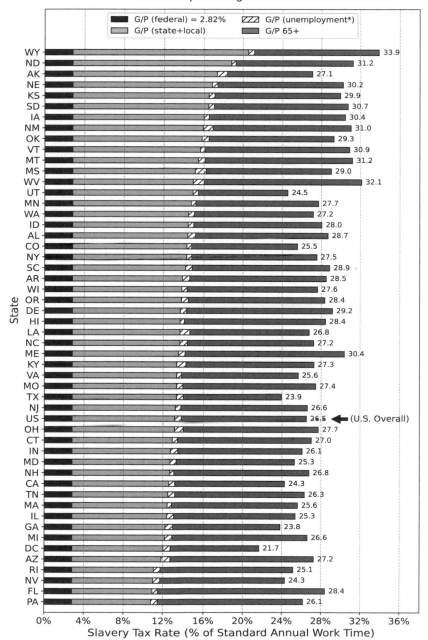

The Infirm

Some individuals will be unable to work due to physical or mental infirmity. If their care is paid for by the government, then they can be tallied as government employees and added to the slavery tax rate.

The Indigent

For those too young to work, say, less than 18 years of age, the laws of some countries may require the parents to provide for them. In the cases that the parents fail to do so, the government may or must do so itself. That same maintenance requirement does not apply to those too old to work in our example, 65+ years of age.

However, it is unreasonable to expect all individuals to have the lifelong knowledge and ability to invest for their retirement with certainty. Retirement investments can be lost due to bad luck, bad judgment, crime, a lack of knowledge and ability, or simply not earning enough to save. As allopolistic losses increase, so too will the proportion of the population that does not earn enough to save for retirement. Unless a culture accepts having the indigent elderly starve to death or die of exposure, the indigent elderly must be supported.

There will also be those of working ages 18 to 64 who cannot work for various reasons. They are or will also be indigent.

An alternative to starving to death is that the indigent commit crimes to survive, even to be imprisoned, where they will be fed and have protection from the elements. In other words, they will be a cost to society regardless. How to support the indigent is a question of which costs less and the culture's mores and laws.

Pensions

Government investment into tightly controlled pension funds could reduce the retirement portion of this tax by the amount of investment returns. Without looking at the numbers, we know that absent allopolistic loss, a government can consolidate large amounts of money and invest with less risk than the private sector. Some government investment organisms appear to function well, such as in the U.S. Railroad Retirement Board.

Medicine

Ultimately, a government, through incentives and law, holds the power to direct medical research and create infrastructure. Large sums of money are involved because most of the population will require medical care at some point in their lives, and the demand for that care will be inelastic. Further, governments may impose regulations for many reasons because medicine involves the population's health and well-being.

A government that regulates the medical field, funds medical research, and that permits its medical industry to focus effort and resources upon extending a debilitated lifespan for profit, as opposed developing cures, has likely permitted allopolies to form in that area.

The Incarcerated and Other Government Wards

The government uses tax money to maintain incarcerated individuals. Therefore, they can be treated as government employees when computing the slavery tax rate, along with any other wards of the government.

QUESTION #7: How many government workers are required for each citizen?

The slavery tax rate was computed for the population that pays for the government. For this text, that population is people aged 18-64 years, less the unemployed. Estimates of the total population $\left(P_{[all]}\right)$ are used here because the government serves the entire population. Viewed another way, the entire population is the load placed upon government resources.

The United States is composed of 50 semi-sovereign states. Data for these states may provide an indication of what is a reasonable government-worker-to-population-member ratio for a given level of government service, for the current circumstances of the United States.

Federal government workers work for the entire population and ostensibly enable the state + local government workers to do their jobs. The number of federal workers for each state is apportioned by the state's total population for 2018 as follows:

$$\frac{G_F}{P_{[all]}} = \frac{5,469,064}{326,687,501} = 0.01674 \; \frac{\text{Federal Gov Workers}}{\text{Population Member}}$$

A plot of the number of government workers (federal + state + local) versus the total population for each State reveals a remarkably consistent overall $\dfrac{G_{F+S+L}}{P_{[all]}}$ ratio around 0.07612* across a wide range of states and state populations, as shown in Figure 6. The population-member-per-government-worker ratio is the inverse, around 13.1 population members to one government worker.

*Note: This regression line is an approximation for visual reference.

*Figure 6: 2018 U.S. Government Workers (Federal+State+Local)
vs Total Population. Federal government workers
apportioned using a $G_F / P_{[all]}$ ratio of 0.01674*

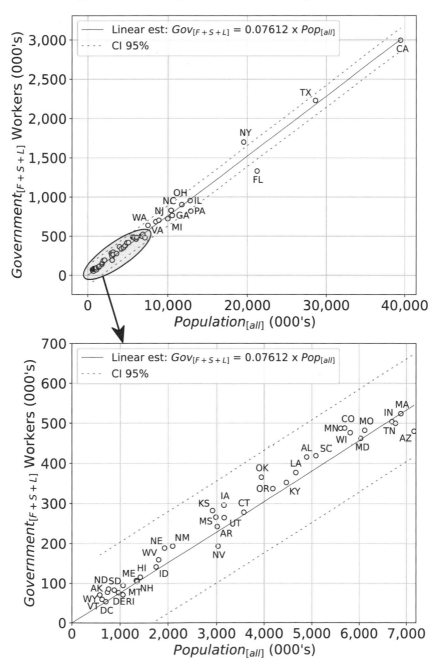

Should there be a government worker for every five citizens? Every ten citizens? Every 100 citizens? Every 1,000 citizens? Common sense and environment would help dictate the answer.

E.g.: If a culture has 40 people, of whom ten are full-time government workers, then

$$\text{STR}_w = \frac{G}{P} = \frac{10}{40} = 25\%$$

That is to say four population members to one government worker. Would there be enough work for the ten full-time government workers to justify forcing the entire population to work 25% of their time, that is 12.5 weeks of the standard work year, to pay for the ten government workers? The ten government workers would likely think so. But what about the other 30 people?

E.g.: A country with hostile neighbors who have armies that will attack if they perceive an opportunity may need to spend time to maintain a military capable of defending the country.

E.g.: A country that is not under threat of attack, but has a large military may, as the accumulation of allopolistic loss increases, turn that military against its own citizens to maintain or to further increase the imposition of allopolistic loss upon the population.

The United States total and state populations, and government employment data for 2018 are shown for reference in Appendix A and Appendix B, respectively.

QUESTION #8: Is a government spending too much?

Allopolists in and with government will defend their interests by saying their expenditures are necessary. However, government expenditures should reduce the amount of time the population is taxed, not increase it.

Government expenditures that increase taxes without an eventual planned return by a greater reduction in taxes, in terms of time, are likely imposing allopolistic losses.

The slavery tax rate provides an objective target for tax reduction.

QUESTION #9: What is the appropriate level of technology a government should provide in the way of government provided technological infrastructure?

The visceral go/no-go point about the level of technology that should be implemented is the amount of time it would return to the population, versus how much time it would cost the population to implement. However, it is not that simple.

As stated by *THEOREM #12: Rate of a Civilization's Technological Development*, the technological level of a society is the starting point for the efforts of individuals. Hence for a society to advance technologically, there will be times when the implementation of technological advances should be made even if there is no time gain or even if there is an initial time loss; that is to say an investment.

That investment decision is also directly affected by *COROLLARY #7: Value Shift from Long to Short Term* which predicts that, with the accumulation allopolistic loss on a culture, comes a shortening of the time frame in which decisions are made.

E.g.:   If the culture's technological level can support a centralized water distribution system, then a government that fails to create such for the population forces people to travel to a river to obtain water. The time the people spend getting water, compared to turning on a faucet, should be added to the tax amount. In this example, the government's failure to create a transportation infrastructure results in the travel time to and from the water source, which can be counted as a tax. Also, if the land supported wells that could be powered by wind-driven pumps, then a centralized water system might not be a good government investment. Electric pumps could also be used, but they might require a centralized electrical distribution system that could, depending on circumstances, greatly improve the quality of life of the population. And so on.

Regardless of the considerations, the plan selected will depend upon whether the cost-benefit analysis is made looking only one year into the future or looking 30 years or 100 years into the future.

E.g.:   The country as a whole will eventually benefit from education and basic research. The plan for subsidizing education will likely vary based upon whether the cost-benefit analysis is made looking only one year into the future or looking 30 or 100 years into the future.

QUESTION #10:   Is a student receiving a government-subsidized education a government employee?

In a public school system, excluding room and board, no. Education is a service provided by the government. The relevant educational staff and facilities are government workers and costs. One student out of 125 in a lecture hall is a minimal cost. However, the outcomes will depend on the implementation.

Per *COROLLARY #9: Technological Advancement Versus the Number of Educated Individuals*, a fully government-subsidized education open to all the population can be an investment in the future of that country. On the other hand, education granted only to a select few can result in the creation of a caste system.

QUESTION #11:   How is non-tax imposed allopolistic loss tallied?

Allopolistic loss can be imposed in a variety of ways. It need not be imposed by government. A private company, enjoying the lack of competition provided by a government's protection may increase consumer prices. An allopoly in the form of a cartel of food distributors can set prices as they see fit. Thus the imposed allopolistic loss is hidden in the price of products and services. Regardless of the imposition method, using the slavery tax rate calculation to compare different periods of time will reveal changes in the imposed tax and costs.

E.g.: To pay for the same amount of electricity (pay the electric bill) as last year, an individual must work (a) the same amount of time as before, (b) more time than before or (c) less time than before.

Resources with Inelastic Demand

Permitting resources with inelastic demand, such as water, roads, shelter, electricity, fuel and other utilities, to fall under unrestrained allopolistic control will, eventually result in increasing allopolistic loss being imposed on the population, according to several theorems covered in this text. Permitting allopolies in these areas to charge allopolistic prices in excess of what would be possible in a competitive environment, or at cost if run by government, is also usually the result of acts or omissions of government, that are themselves likely the result of allopolistic activity.

Such excess prices in these areas should be considered a tax imposed by the government. Granted, there are market considerations. However, the key here is that imposed allopolistic loss on resources and infrastructure with inelastic demand through action or inaction of government should be tallied as an imposed tax.

QUESTION #12:   Is a government too intrusive?

Generally, infrastructure with inelastic demand as well as inherently governmental functions, such as law enforcement and military, is usually best run by government. The other part of this question is more complex because it involves human nature. It is predicted by *COROLLARY #2: Reduction of Target Allopoly Secrecy* that governing allopolies will strive to reduce the secrecy of their subject allopolies; in other words, reduce their privacy. Being under surveillance, either recorded or direct, reduces the time available to each individual and, therefore, is a tax in terms of that person's time.

Violation of a person's or allopoly's privacy is a means of reducing the individual's or allopoly's ability to defend themselves from the imposition of allopolistic loss.

E.g.: A government implements a system that tracks who communicates with whom be it postal letters, phone or computers, records all phone communications, all bank account and credit activity and all travel via cell phone and integrated GPS, facial recognition and license plate readers. The reason for the system's creation was to combat terrorism originating in foreign countries.

It is subsequently discovered that these data collection cyber-weapons have been primarily aimed at the country's own citizens. A citizen proposes legislation that would purge the system of information on its own citizens and prohibit further collection.

An allopoly of government law enforcement and security personnel that uses this system for personal gain, searches the database to determine the citizen's political contacts and sources of financial support. The searchers concluded that sufficient legal pressure would bankrupt the citizen and her supporters, the other leaders of the political movement. The government allopoly searches the database for a time and location at which the citizen usually does not have an alibi, there are no cameras that the government allopoly cannot control, and there will likely not be witnesses. A crime and discovery method is fabricated and executed.

Once such a system is in place, this method can be used to coerce individuals to give false testimony against the accused citizen either by threat of doing the same to the individual or the individual's family and friends. It further lends credibility to the corrupt government as it does not need to rely on the incarcerated, that is jail-house informants to obtain convictions. Other branches of government that are unaware of this activity, such as judges, become unwitting collaborators.

Attempts by the citizen to discover the source and the means of the accusation are met with claims by the government that the information is classified and cannot be released. The population then begins to live in fear of their government.

Time and resources the individual must spend, unprovoked, to keep a government from decreasing their quality of life should also be counted as a tax. These types of taxes are, per ***COROLLARY #8: Multiplicative and Cascade Effect of Allopolistic Loss***, a multiplicative and cascading imposition of allopolistic loss. The reason is that the government is using the time individuals spend to support it to take actions that cause the individuals to spend more time defending themselves from the government. This imposition of allopolistic loss upon the individual also imposes an opportunity cost. Such allopolistic losses are generally the result of a corrupt government attempting to keep or gain power.

Defensive individual allopolistic costs are further compounded by a government's failure to provide needed infrastructure and security. Accumulated, direct and opportunity time costs tallied as imposed taxes provide the means to measure allopolistic loss imposed upon the individual. The slavery tax rate provides a standard interpretation of the measure.

E.g.: A government creates a licensing scheme where licenses eventually expire. Individuals then must go to the government offices to renew that license. If the government does not provide the infrastructure for travel, and the travel to and from the government office takes the individual six hours, then that time is also a tax to be added to the tally of imposed taxes, in addition to the license fee, and measured against the slavery tax rate.

As governments generally have an allopoly on coercive force, they may impose allopolistic loss via an infinite variety of allopolistic behaviors.

E.g.: Denial of access to infrastructure, such as access to transportation, denial of travel permits, etc., may effectively imprison an individual due to time, costs and opportunity costs. Attempts to conceal the intrusion by forcing individuals to use more time-consuming means of travel are tallied as an imposed tax by using the difference of the individual's time and the two travel methods, along with the associated opportunity costs. The slavery tax rate provides the yardstick to measure the intrusion into the individual's life.

Alongside taxes, a government's ubiquitous intrusion into the life of individuals is its legal system, which directly affects individuals. Legal proceedings by a government may impose an allopolistic loss in terms of accumulated time (money and resources), actual time in terms of the legal process, opportunity costs in terms of what the individual could have been otherwise doing and the benefits that would have resulted. Such allopolistic impositions by government are taxes.

Infinite forms of government actions can be used as examples, but the analysis is the same because the measure is the individual's time, and the yardstick of intrusiveness is the slavery tax rate.

E.g.: A government has a legal system based upon the premise that individuals are presumed innocent until proven guilty in a court of law. In such a system, an arrest by the government is merely an accusation. However, the individual must spend their time to defend themselves. If such a government fails to prove guilt, then all the individual's time, such as legal expenses (accumulated time), incarceration, loss of employment (opportunity), etc., are taxes imposed upon the individual. Thus, the use of time as a metric reveals the extent of the imposition of allopolistic loss by the government upon the individual.

Because governments both promote and inhibit behaviors, **THEOREM #3: Preference to Form Allopolies with Governing Allopolies** can manifest itself in the negative by a government failing to inhibit behavior and thereby tacitly expanding its ability to impose allopolistic loss indirectly.

E.g.:   In a criminal prosecution, a government has laws that require its law enforcement arm to collect and provide all exculpatory evidence to the accused for their defense. However, the law enforcement branch repeatedly fails to do so. By not prosecuting the particular law enforcement personnel and prosecutors for failing to do so, there is only gain for violating the laws. Thus the government has circumvented its own rules. The time and resources spent by the individual defending themselves as well as the time lost due to the imposition of any criminal penalties if the case is lost are imposed allopolistic losses or tax, upon the individual's time.

E.g.:   A government has a legal system based upon the premise that individuals are presumed innocent until proven guilty in a court of law. As stated in the example on the previous page, in such a system, an arrest is merely an accusation. If such a government permits employers to inquire whether a prospective employee has ever been arrested as opposed to having been convicted of a crime, that government is tacitly expanding its power by circumventing its own tenet. Having failed to prove the individual guilty, the government may still impose a similar penalty on the individual's ability to find work in the future. The use of time as a metric of allopolistic loss could capture the opportunity cost and the individual's lost time, counting it as an imposed tax.

SUMMARY

The slavery tax rate is an objective demarcation of the moment when government imposed or sanctioned taxes and costs turns its citizens into slaves. That point arises naturally from the calculation of the slavery tax rate itself.

The slavery tax rate is a time-based metric that can be used for comparisons across time without adjustment.

The classification or stratification of government type (federal, state, local, etc.), or the tax type (sales, VAT, property, etc.) is irrelevant. All government-associated taxes, surcharges, and costs imposed upon the individual directly or indirectly should be tallied to determine an individual's position with respect to the slavery tax rate.

The slavery tax rate calculation provides a visible measure of government dysfunction.

The slavery tax rate calculation makes visible the use of taxes by higher government levels to usurp power from lower government levels.

In its essence, Allopoly Theory is devoid of legality or morality. It is simply the study of economics as practiced.

DATA CONSISTENCY CHECKS

Federal Government Employment Data

The total federal employment data published by the U.S. Bureau of Labor Statistics [59] were compared to the Federal Workforce Data published by the U.S. Office of Personnel Management.[64] Neither set contains employment data of active military, which were obtained from the U.S. Department of Defense.[60]

The U.S. Bureau of Labor Statistics' estimates of federal government workers for years 2010 through 2018 were, on average, of two million people higher than the data published by the U.S. Office of Personnel Management, as shown in Table 5.

Table 5:   Comparison of Total Federal Employee Count published data: U.S. Bureau of Labor Statistics CE series data versus U.S. Office of Personnel Management Federal Workforce data and U.S. Department of Defense.

Year	U.S. Bureau of Labor Statistics (BLS)	U.S. Office of Personnel Management (OPM)	Difference: BLS – OPM	Percent Difference BLS vs OPM	U.S. Department of Defense (DoD)	Total Federal Employees BLS + DoD
2010	4,205,800	2,113,210	2,092,590	99.0%	1,458,701	5,664,501
2011	4,178,200	2,130,289	2,047,911	96.1%	1,453,437	5,631,637
2012	4,142,000	2,110,221	2,031,779	96.3%	1,429,878	5,571,878
2013	4,038,800	2,067,262	1,971,538	95.4%	1,410,749	5,449,549
2014	4,027,800	2,045,707	1,982,093	96.9%	1,365,728	5,393,528
2015	4,060,100	2,058,924	2,001,176	97.2%	1,340,533	5,400,633
2016	4,112,100	2,097,038	2,015,062	96.1%	1,328,194	5,440,294
2017	4,103,700	2,087,747	2,015,953	96.6%	1,335,122	5,438,822
2018	4,123,900	2,100,802	2,023,098	96.3%	1,345,164	5,469,064
Average			**2,020,133**	**96.6%**		

U.S. Bureau of Labor Statistics Current Employment Survey Data Exclusions (CE Series)

CE series national federal government employment (90910000) covers civilian employees only; military personnel are excluded (civilians who work for the DoD are included). Employees of the Central Intelligence Agency, the National Security Agency, the National Imagery and Mapping Agency, and the Defense Intelligence Agency are also excluded.

U.S. Office of Personnel Management Data Exclusions

The EHRI-SDM covers most of the non-Postal Federal Executive Branch. Coverage is limited to Federal civilian employees with the following inclusions or exclusions:

Executive Branch coverage includes all agencies except the following: Board of Governors of the Federal Reserve, Central Intelligence Agency, Defense Intelligence Agency, Foreign Service personnel at the State Department (included until March 2006), National Geospatial-Intelligence Agency, National Security Agency, Office of the Director of National Intelligence, Office of the Vice President, Postal Regulatory Commission, Tennessee Valley Authority, U.S. Postal Service, White House Office. Other exclusions include: foreign nationals overseas, Public Health Service's Commissioned Officer Corps, non-appropriated fund employees.

There appeared to be a difference between the U.S. Office of Personnel Management published data files and its Fedscope interactive cube viewer at the time these data were retrieved, shown in Appendix C.

The U.S. Bureau of Labor Statistics' CE series federal employment estimates [59] were used for the examples in this text.

State Government Employment Data

The U.S. Bureau of Labor Statistics state government employment data [61] were compared to the state employee counts published by each state in their Comprehensive Annual Financial Reports (CAFR).[65] The U.S. Bureau of Labor Statistics state government employee estimates summed for all 50 states and the District of Columbia for years 2010 through 2018, were an average of 1.9 million government workers higher than that of each state's Comprehensive Annual Financial Report as shown in Table 6.

Because sampling error may accumulate when summing the U.S. Bureau of Labor Statistics SM series state employment values to the national level, the median differences and percent differences are also shown in Table 6 for comparison. The government employment data for individual states are shown in Appendix D.

Table 6: Comparison of State Employee Count published data:
U.S. Bureau of Labor Statistics (BLS) SM Series
data* vs State Comprehensive Annual Reports (CAFR)
for All States and the District of Columbia.

Data	2010	2011	2012	2013	2014	2015	2016	2017	2018
BLS SM sum	5,359,700	5,335,800	5,323,300	5,344,300	5,374,700	5,380,400	5,401,300	5,435,600	5,437,700
CAFR sum	3,531,258	3,495,310	3,459,853	3,398,091	3,390,699	3,402,609	3,413,016	3,430,048	3,427,080
Sum Diff.	1,828,442	1,840,490	1,863,447	1,946,210	1,984,001	1,977,791	1,988,284	2,005,552	2,010,620
Sum Pct. Diff.	51.8%	52.7%	53.9%	57.3%	58.5%	58.1%	58.3%	58.5%	58.7%
Mean Diff.	35,852	36,088	36,538	38,161	38,902	38,780	38,986	39,325	39,424
Mean Pct. Diff.	80.3%	82.7%	85.3%	89.5%	91.4%	91.0%	92.1%	92.5%	92.4%
Median Diff.	27,675	28,709	28,873	30,486	31,641	25,755	27,240	27,290	27,542
Median Pct. Diff.	54.9%	54.3%	56.4%	60.2%	57.3%	55.9%	60.7%	55.1%	63.2%

*Note: The U.S. Bureau of labor statistics website states:

"The state and area estimates use smaller amounts of sample by industry than the national industry estimates. This increases the error component associated with state and metropolitan level estimates.

For this reason, aggregating state data to the national level will also sum this error component, resulting in different estimates of U.S. employment, hours, and earnings. Summed state level CES estimates should not be compared with national CES estimates."

U.S. Bureau of Labor Statistics Current Employment Survey Data Exclusions (SM Series)

The U.S. Bureau of Labor Statistics inclusion and exclusion information regarding their SM series for state and local government employment could not be confirmed by press time.

Individual State Comprehensive Annual Financial Report State Government Employee Exclusions

The employee inclusions and exclusions of the state's Comprehensive Annual Financial Reports differ from each other. For this comparison, separate counts for temporary or part-time workers were added to the state government employee totals. The individual state Comprehensive Annual Financial Reports used are identified in Appendix E.

The U.S. Bureau of Labor Statistics' SM series for state and local government employee estimates[61] were used for the examples in this text.

REFERENCES
(* General reading or viewing)

[1]   Skinner, B.F. (1937) Two types of conditioned reflex: a reply to Konorski and Miller. *The Journal of General Psychology*, 16:272–279. Retrieved from https://doi.org/10.1080/00221309.1937.9917951.

[2]   Varian, Hal. (1992) *Microeconomic Analysis*. (3rd ed.). (Chapter 14: Monopoly). W. W. Norton & Co. ISBN: 0-393-95735-7.

[3]   Madison, James. (1788, January 23). The Same Subject Continued: The Powers Conferred by the Constitution Further Considered. (Federalist Paper 43. Miscellaneous power 2). *The Independent Journal*. Retrieved from https://guides.loc.gov/federalist-papers/text-41-50#s-lg-box-wrapper-25493407 .*

[4]   Jehle, Geoffrey A. (1991) *Advanced Microeconomic Theory*. (Chapter 3: Consumer Theory I). Prentice-Hall Inc. ISBN: 0-13-010315-2.

[5]   Buchanan, James M., Tullock, Gordon. (1962) *The Calculus of Consent: Logical Foundations of Constitutional Democracy*. Ann Arbor Paperbacks. ISBN: 0-86597-218-4.*

[6]   Ricardo, David. (1817) *On the Principles of Political Economy and Taxation*. (1st ed.). London: John Murray.*

[7]   The Code of Hammurabi. (circa 1792-1750 B.C.) *Law #3*. Retrieved from https://avalon.law.yale.edu/ancient/hamframe.asp .*

[8]   Doyle, Charles. (2020). Federal Conspiracy Law: A Brief Overview. *Congressional Research Service Report No. R41223*. Retrieved from https://crsreports.congress.gov/product/pdf/download/R/R41223/R41223.pdf .*

[9]   Relyea, Harold C. (1988) The Coming of Secret Law. *Government Information Quarterly*, volume 5, issue 2, pp 97-116. https://doi.org/10.1016/0740-624X(88)90068-8 .*

[10] U.S. Constitution. Amendment III. Retrieved from https://www.archives.gov/founding-docs/bill-of-rights-transcript .*

[11] U.S. Constitution. Amendment IV. Retrieved from https://www.archives.gov/founding-docs/bill-of-rights-transcript .*

[12]   U.S. Constitution. Amendment I. Retrieved from
       https://www.archives.gov/founding-docs/bill-of-rights-transcript .*

[13]   Luksik, Peg. (1992) (Writer, Speaker) *Who Controls Our Children?*
       [Motion Picture - Documentary] Retrieved from
       https://www.youtube.com/watch?v=NxtVAJN67Vk .*

[14]   Social Security Administration. (2020). *Measures of Central
       Tendency for Wage Data.* Retrieved from
       https://www.ssa.gov/OACT/COLA/central.html .*

[15]   The Committee On The Judiciary House Of Representatives (2019,
       December 01). *Federal Rules Of Civil Procedure,* (Rule 23, Class
       Actions). Retrieved from:
       https://www.uscourts.gov/rules-policies/current-rules-practice-
       procedure/federal-rules-civil-procedure .*

[16]   Spengler, Oswald. (1926-1928) *The Decline of the West.* (2 vols.).
       Alfred A. Knoppf, Inc.*

[17]   Bowdon, Bob. (2009) (Writer/Producer/Director). *The Cartel.*
       [Motion Picture - Documentary] Available from
       https://www.amazon.com/Cartel-Bob-Bowdon/dp/B004CWJ24C or
       http://www.amazon.com ASIN: B0048ASB0O.*

[18]   Holcomb, Kovandzic and Williams. (2011). Civil asset forfeiture,
       equitable sharing, and policing for profit in the United States.
       Journal of Criminal Justice, volume 39, pp 273-285. Retrieved from
       https://libres.uncg.edu/ir/asu/f/Holcomb_Kovandzic_Williams_2011_
       Civil%20asset%20forfeiture.pdf .*

[19]   Civil Rights Division, U.S. Department of Justice. (2015, March 04).
       Investigation of the Ferguson Police Department. Retrieved from
       https://www.justice.gov/sites/default/files/opa/press-releases/attachme
       nts/2015/03/04/ferguson_police_department_report.pdf. *

[20]   Lipton, E., Hakim, L. (2013, October 18). Lobbying Bonanza as
       Firms Try to Influence European Union. *New York Times.* Retrieved
       from http://www.nytimes.com/2013/10/19/world/europe/lobbying-
       bonanza-as-firms-try-to-influence-european-union.html .*

[21]   Posse Comitatus Act. U.S. Code, Title 18, Part I, Chapter 67, § 1385. Retrieved from https://uscode.house.gov/view.xhtml?req=(title:18%20section:1385%20edition:prelim)%20OR%20(granuleid:USC-prelim-title18-section1385)&f=treesort&edition=prelim&num=0&jumpTo=true .*

[22]   Sulla, Lucius. (circa 81 B.C.) *Lex Cornelia de Maiestate* or *Leges Corneliae*. Ancient Roman Law.

[23]   U.S. Constitution. Amendment II. Retrieved from https://www.archives.gov/founding-docs/bill-of-rights-transcript .*

[24]   The Federal Constitutional Court of Germany. BVerfG, Judgment of the Second Senate of 03 March 2009 - 2 BvC 3/07 - paras. (1-166). Retrieved on from http://www.bverfg.de/e/cs20090303_2bvc000307en.html .*

[25]   Racketeer Influenced and Corrupt Organizations (RICO). (8 USC Ch. 96). Retrieved from https://uscode.house.gov/view.xhtml?path=/prelim@title18/part1/chapter96&edition=prelim .*

[26]   Adams, Brooks. (1896) *The Law of Civilization and Decay; an Essay on History*. Books for Libraries Press.*

[27]   American Bar Association. (2015) *Model Rules of Professional Conduct*. (Rule 5.4: Professional Independence of a Lawyer) ABA Publishing. ISBN: 978-1-63425-093-1. Retrieved from http://www.americanbar.org/groups/professional_responsibility/publications/model_rules_of_professional_conduct/rule_5_4_professional_independence_of_a_lawyer.html .*

[28]   Kusserow, Richard P. (1991, November) State Prohibitions On Hospital Employment Of Physicians. *Department of Health and Human Ser*vices, Office Of Inspector General. OEI-01-91-00770. Retrieved from http://oig.hhs.gov/oei/reports/oei-01-91-00770.pdf .*

[29]   Moran, Lyle. (2020, August 14) Utah embraces nonlawyer ownership of law firms as part of broad access-to-justice reforms. *American Bar Association Journal*. Retrieved from https://www.abajournal.com/web/article/utah-embraces-nonlawyer-ownership-of-law-firms-as-part-of-broad-reforms .*

[30] Bush, Vannevar. (1945, July) *Science: The Endless Frontier, A report to the president on postwar scientific research.* (Reprinted 1960) National Science Foundation. Retrieved from http://dx.doi.org/10.5962/bhl.title.5727 .*

[31] Myhrvold, Nathan. (2016, February). Even Genius Needs a Benefactor. *Scientific American p17.*

[32] Toynbee, Arnold. (1934-1961) *A Study of History.* (12 vols.) Oxford University Press.*

[33] Baruzzi, Sofia. (2020, October 12) Why is China Introducing New Export Controls? *China Briefing. Dezan Shira & Associates.* Retrieved on December 12, 2020 from: https://www.china-briefing.com/news/chinas-new-export-control-law-restrictions-imposed-23-items-technology/ .*

[34] Monopolies And Combinations In Restraint Of Trade. (15 USC Chapter 1, §1 to §38). Retrieved from https://uscode.house.gov/browse/prelim@title15&edition=prelim .*

[35] Henn, Harry G., Alexander, John R. (1983) *Laws of Corporations: And Other Business Enterprises (3rd edition.).* (Chapter 1B: Historical Background, and Chapter 9: Purposes (Or Objects) & Powers). West Academic Publishing. ISBN: 0-314-69870-1.

[36] United States Supreme Court. (2010, January 10) Citizens United vs. Federal Election Commission (558 U.S. 310). Retrieved from http://www.supremecourt.gov/opinions/09pdf/08-205.pdf (186 pages).*

[37] United States Supreme Court. (2014, April 02) McCutcheon et al. vs. Federal Election Commission (134 S. Ct. 1434). Retrieved from http://www.supremecourt.gov/opinions/13pdf/12-536_e1pf.pdf (94 pages).*

[38] Jones, Huw (2014, July 30). Bank of England imposes seven-year bonus clawback on errant bankers. *Reuters Business News.* Retrieved from https://www.reuters.com/article/uk-boe-banking-bonuses/bank-of-england-imposes-seven-year-bonus-clawback-on-errant-bankers-idUKKBN0FZ0SB20140730 .*

[39]   Cho, Jeh-Hyun, Hwang, Iny, Hyun, Jeong-Hoon, Shin, Jae Yong. (2020, Spring). Compensation Consultant Fees and CEO Pay. *Journal of Management Accounting Research,* volume 32, number 1, pp 51–78. Retrieved from https://doi.org/10.2308/jmar-52434 .*

[40]   Hardin, Garrett. (1968) The Tragedy of the Commons. *Science. Vol. 162 no. 3859 pp. 1243-1248.* Retrieved from https://pages.mtu.edu/~asmayer/rural_sustain/governance/Hardin%201968.pdf .*

[41]   Smith, Adam. (1776). *The Wealth of Nations.* Penguin Books. Books I-III. ISBN: 0-14-043208-6.*

[42]   Childe, Gordon. (1936). *Man Makes Himself.* (Chapter 5: The Neolithic Revolution) New American Library.*

[43]   Quigley, Carroll. (1961). *The Evolution of Civilizations.* Liberty Fund, Inc. ISBN: 978-0-913966-57-0.*

[44]   Myerson, Roger B. (1991). *Game Theory: Analysis of Conflict.* (Chapter 3: Equilibria of Strategic Form Games) Harvard University Press. ISBN: 0-674-34115-5.

[45]   Fudenberg D., Tirole J. (1991). *Game Theory.* (Chapter IV: Dynamic Games of Incomplete Information)The MIT Press. ISBN: 0-262-06141-4.

[46]   Veblen, T. B. (1899). *The Theory of the Leisure Class. An Economic Study of Institutions.* The Macmillan Company, London.*

[47]   Merriam-Webster. (n.d.). Corruption. In Merriam-Webster.com dictionary. Retrieved from https://www.merriam-webster.com/dictionary/corruption .*

[48]   Appointment of Inspector General; supervision; removal; political activities; appointment of Assistant Inspector General for Auditing and Assistant Inspector General for Investigations. (5a U.S. Code § 3). Retrieved from https://uscode.house.gov/view.xhtml?req=granuleid:USC-prelim-title5a-node20-section3&num=0&edition=prelim .* Office of Inspectors General list at: https://www.ignet.gov/content/inspectors-general-directory .*

[49]   The Privacy Act of 1974. (5 U.S. Code § 552a). Retrieved from https://www.archives.gov/about/laws/privacy-act-1974.html .*

[50] Human Rights Watch. (2018, January 01). *Dark Side: Secret Origins of Evidence in US Criminal Cases*. ISBN: 978-1-6231-35645. Retrieved on November 21, 2020 from https://www.hrw.org/report/2018/01/09/dark-side/secret-origins-evidence-us-criminal-cases .*

[51] Ryscavage, Paul. (1986, July 01). Reconciling divergent trends in real income. Bureau of Labor Statistics. *Monthly Labor Statistics, July 01, 1986. pp 24-29*. Retrieved from https://www.bls.gov/opub/mlr/1986/07/art3full.pdf .*

[52] Patterson, Orlando. (1982, 2018). *Slavery and Social Death, A Comparative Study*. Harvard University Press. ISBN: 978-0-674-81082-2.*

[53] McKitrick, Eric L. [Editor] (1963) *Slavery Defended: the Views of the Old South*. Prentice-Hall Inc. Library of Congress catalog card number: 63-12270.*

[54] Watson, Judy A. (1998, January 30) County Government Abolishment. *Connecticut Assembly Office of Legal Research. Research paper: 98-R-0086*. Retrieved from https://www.cga.ct.gov/PS98/rpt%5Colr%5Chtm/98-R-0086.htm .*

[55] U.S. Bureau of the Census (2017). 2017 Census of Governments – Organization, table 2. Local Governments by Type and State: 2017 [CG1700ORG02]. Retrieved on November 07, 2020 from https://www.census.gov/data/tables/2017/econ/gus/2017-governments.html .*

[56] U.S. Bureau of the Census. (2020) National Population by Characteristics: 2010-2019. The ACS DP05 tables of 5-year estimates. Retrieved on November 07, 2020 from https://data.census.gov/cedsci .

[57] U.S. Bureau of the Census. (2020) Population, Population Change, and Estimated Components of Population Change: April 1, 2010 to July 1, 2019 (NST-EST2019-alldata). Retrieved on November 07, 2020 from http://www2.census.gov/programs-surveys/popest/datasets/2010-2019/national/totals/nst-est2019-alldata.csv .

[58] U.S. Bureau of Labor Statistics. (2020). The *Local Area Unemployment Statistics (LA)* series for Statewide Unemployment. Retrieved on November 08, 2020 from https://download.bls.gov/pub/time.series/la .

[59]   U.S. Bureau of Labor Statistics. (2020) The *Employment, Hours, And Earnings - National (CE)* series for Federal Government (90910000). Retrieved on November 08, 2020 from https://download.bls.gov/pub/time.series/ce .

[60]   U.S. Department of Defense, DoD Personnel (2020). Workforce Reports & Publications. *DMDC Website Location Report* for September of each year. Retrieved on November 08, 2020 from https://www.dmdc.osd.mil/appj/dwp/dwp_reports.jsp .*

[61]   U.S. Bureau of Labor Statistics. (2020). The *State And Area Employment, Hours And Earnings (SM)* series for State Government (90920000), Local Government (90930000), Total State and Local Government (90940000), and District of Columbia Government (90940001). Retrieved on November 08, 2020 from https://download.bls.gov/pub/time.series/sm .

[62]   U.S. Internal Revenue Service. (2020). Statistics of Income - Historic Table 2, Tax Year 2018. Retrieved from https://www.irs.gov/pub/irs-soi/18in55cm.xlsx .*

[63]   U.S. Constitution. Article 1, Section 8, Clause 17. Retrieved from https://www.archives.gov/founding-docs/constitution-transcript .*

[64]   U.S. Office of Personnel Management (2020). Federal Workforce Data.
   • Fedscope Interactive data retrieved on December 05, 2020 from https://www.fedscope.opm.gov/employment.asp .*
   • Data sets retrieved on May 24, 2020 from https://www.opm.gov/data/index.aspx .

[65]   Each state publishes its own Comprehensive Annual Financial Report (CAFR) that can be found on each state's official website. The listing in Appendix E identifies the Fiscal Year (FY) of the CAFR used for each state, and the page containing the state employee count. *

APPENDIX A:
2018 U.S. POPULATION, INCOME, FEDERAL GOVERNMENT WORKERS AND UNEMPLOYMENT

Federal Government Workers [59][60] $\left(G_F\right)$	Total Population [57] $\left(P_{[all]}\right)$	Population Ages 18-64 years [56] $\left(P_{[18-64]}\right)$	Unemployed [58] $\left(P_{[unemp]}\right)$	Population Ages 65+ years [56] $\left(P_{[65+]}\right)$	Individual Income [62] ($000)
5,469,064	326,687,501	200,111,209	6,385,787	49,238,581	11,769,733,622

Note: Data source references are enclosed in brackets [ ].

APPENDIX B:
2018 STATE POPULATION, INCOME, STATE + LOCAL GOVERNMENT WORKERS AND UNEMPLOYMENT

State	State + Local Government Workers [61] $\left(G_{SL}\right)$	Total Population [57] $\left(P_{[all]}\right)$	Population Ages 18-64 years [56] $\left(P_{[18-64]}\right)$	Unemployed [58] $\left(P_{[U]}\right)$	Population Ages 65+ years [56] $\left(P_{[65+]}\right)$	Individual Income [62] ($000)
Alabama	333,800	4,887,681	2,982,055	85,782	783,832	125,765,499
Alaska	65,500	735,139	473,950	22,761	78,428	25,462,885
Arizona	360,300	7,158,024	4,154,582	162,065	1,158,320	212,186,534
Arkansas	192,000	3,009,733	1,797,192	49,310	487,536	76,610,435
California	2,335,300	39,461,588	24,759,648	820,096	5,315,457	1,642,557,700
Colorado	392,700	5,691,287	3,530,684	97,163	740,638	231,052,124
Connecticut	218,200	3,571,520	2,241,299	78,773	587,580	180,629,965
Delaware	60,500	965,479	578,940	18,231	167,129	33,418,386
District of Columbia	42,200	701,547	481,049	23,036	81,712	37,518,014
Florida	975,400	21,244,317	12,385,211	364,881	4,064,376	761,164,251
Georgia	588,800	10,511,131	6,443,900	200,434	1,352,289	314,765,707
Hawaii	91,900	1,420,593	869,573	16,928	245,955	47,432,508
Idaho	112,100	1,750,536	994,832	24,921	253,801	50,415,355
Illinois	740,700	12,723,071	8,000,033	279,152	1,894,903	495,222,371
Indiana	391,800	6,695,497	4,067,070	117,858	996,063	197,897,138
Iowa	243,000	3,148,618	1,889,155	44,252	513,312	98,592,151
Kansas	233,300	2,911,359	1,755,454	48,618	437,777	93,187,843
Kentucky	277,400	4,461,153	2,736,676	89,180	691,509	116,083,699
Louisiana	298,900	4,659,690	2,878,435	102,502	676,707	120,887,846
Maine	84,800	1,339,057	818,976	22,529	259,176	41,692,669
Maryland	361,200	6,035,802	3,783,921	127,034	875,337	249,747,949

State	State + Local Government Workers [61] (G_{SL})	Total Population [57] $(P_{[all]})$	Population Ages 18-64 years [56] $(P_{[18-64]})$	Unemployed [58] $(P_{[U]})$	Population Ages 65+ years [56] $(P_{[65+]})$	Individual Income [62] ($000)
Massachusetts	408,800	6,882,635	4,372,072	127,203	1,078,224	349,848,908
Michigan	556,100	9,984,072	6,140,446	203,354	1,620,944	321,891,306
Minnesota	393,700	5,606,249	3,405,639	90,280	830,112	220,520,489
Mississippi	215,700	2,981,020	1,818,976	61,454	449,478	63,895,200
Missouri	379,900	6,121,623	3,723,307	96,438	981,692	185,104,199
Montana	77,100	1,060,665	630,317	19,266	183,823	32,460,410
Nebraska	156,400	1,925,614	1,146,162	29,930	286,080	61,922,959
Nevada	142,700	3,027,341	1,810,322	66,792	438,051	107,601,110
New Hampshire	82,300	1,353,465	853,075	19,576	227,984	58,665,452
New Jersey	555,000	8,886,025	5,531,580	181,724	1,376,863	412,392,335
New Mexico	158,400	2,092,741	1,256,755	45,914	341,515	52,734,420
New York	1,372,300	19,530,351	12,408,131	394,170	3,068,689	881,433,441
North Carolina	655,800	10,381,615	6,292,010	198,419	1,570,998	311,345,493
North Dakota	73,200	758,080	468,573	10,384	109,910	27,029,536
Ohio	707,200	11,676,341	7,130,850	259,066	1,892,861	365,599,555
Oklahoma	299,300	3,940,235	2,370,201	63,045	589,230	103,692,401
Oregon	266,700	4,181,886	2,531,219	84,967	682,546	142,960,496
Pennsylvania	606,100	12,800,922	7,885,990	272,929	2,229,861	456,227,853
Rhode Island	53,800	1,058,287	673,532	22,076	174,210	38,073,358
South Carolina	333,900	5,084,156	3,030,591	80,882	829,083	143,308,043
South Dakota	68,300	878,698	514,415	14,093	136,808	29,038,106
Tennessee	386,600	6,771,631	4,104,482	114,373	1,045,213	200,683,837
Texas	1,750,400	28,628,666	17,254,695	531,572	3,337,814	936,014,638
Utah	211,800	3,153,550	1,806,032	47,679	320,269	99,447,546
Vermont	49,200	624,358	393,081	8,804	113,550	21,620,262
Virginia	543,200	8,501,286	5,316,101	131,502	1,230,246	330,642,466
Washington	512,500	7,523,869	4,587,962	169,432	1,073,499	329,133,115
West Virginia	129,100	1,804,291	1,110,962	40,870	344,719	42,541,063
Wisconsin	379,200	5,807,406	3,564,756	93,554	924,695	199,174,131
Wyoming	61,200	577,601	356,340	11,352	87,777	22,175,102

Note: Data source references are enclosed in brackets [ ].

APPENDIX C:
U.S. OFFICE OF PERSONNEL MANAGEMENT FEDERAL EMPLOYMENT DATA REFERENCE AND COMPARISON

U.S. Office of Personnel Management Federal Employment Data Files

Year-Month	Employment Data Zip File	Employment Listing File Within the Zip File	Employment Listing File Employment	OPM Fedscope Interactive Cube Employment	Difference
2010-09	c21d50d7-9b48-432c-a03e-96d5fb93f5fa.zip	FACTDATA_SEP2010.TXT	2,113,210	2,113,210	0
2011-09	caac291b-001d-4568-a8be-96215c319fd4.zip	FACTDATA_SEP2011.TXT	2,130,289	2,130,289	0
2012-09	2b43e513-cbfa-4eb5-ae9a-20e718ef1f4e.zip	FACTDATA_SEP2012.TXT	2,110,221	2,110,221	0
2013-09	55974d49-94f0-43e7-acf3-77bf864e802a.zip	FACTDATA_SEP2013.TXT	2,067,262	2,067,262	0
2014-09	f5e03461-5674-4fbe-8538-10a77e7a2739.zip	FACTDATA_SEP2014.TXT	2,045,707	2,045,707	0
2015-09	**de1dd3f7-0c39-46ab-a1c6-848be284358b.zip**	**FACTDATA_SEP2015.TXT**	**2,058,924**	**2,071,716**	**(12,792)**
2016-09	ae0351fd-58d1-47d5-b1aa-2ca3bf977d30.zip	FACTDATA_SEP2016.TXT	2,097,038	2,097,038	0
2017-09	7a0bf199-6c16-4131-92d1-485b18f7878a.zip	FACTDATA_SEP2017.TXT	2,087,747	2,087,747	0
2018-09	cc43dc51-3564-4b1f-abee-6511b43b7738.zip	FACTDATA_SEP2018.TXT	2,100,802	2,100,802	0

U.S. Office of Personnel Management Federal Employment Interactive Data Cube for 2015-09

Employment - September 2015 ► Agency - All ► Location - All ► Age - All ► Education Level - All ► Gender - All ► General Schedule and Equivalent Grade (GSEG) - All ►

Employment - September 2015
Agency - All
Location - All
Age - All
Education Level - All
Gender - All
General Schedule and Equiv...
Length of Service - All
Occupation - All
Occupational Category - All
Pay Plan and Grade - All
Salary Level - All
STEM & Health Occupations
Supervisory Status - All
Type of Appointment - All
Work Schedule - All
Work Status - All
MEASURES

Employment as values	United States	U.S. Territories	Foreign Countries	Unspecified	Location - All
Cabinet Level Agencies	1,857,771	11,693	27,403	884	1,897,751
Large Independent Agencies (1000 or more employees)	159,045	611	1,706	59	161,421
Medium Independent Agencies (100-999 employees)	10,927	NA	35	NA	10,970
Small Independent Agencies (less than 100 employees)	1,550	NA	24	NA	1,574
Agency - All	**2,029,293**	**12,311**	**29,168**	**944**	**2,071,716**

APPENDIX D:
COMPARISON OF STATE GOVERNMENT EMPLOYMENT DATA BETWEEN U.S. BUREAU OF LABOR STATISTICS SM SERIES (BLS) AND INDIVIDUAL STATE 2019 COMPREHENSIVE ANNUAL FINANCIAL REPORTS (CAFR)

State	Data	2010	2011	2012	2013	2014	2015	2016	2017	2018
Alabama (AL)	U.S. BLS	114,800	113,800	111,200	112,200	113,800	114,500	114,700	115,700	117,000
	State CAFR	33,236	33,110	32,970	31,719	32,305	32,997	31,047	30,918	30,736
	Diff	81,564	80,690	78,230	80,481	81,495	81,503	83,653	84,782	86,264
	Percent Diff	245.4%	243.7%	237.3%	253.7%	252.3%	247.0%	269.4%	274.2%	280.7%
Alaska (AK)	U.S. BLS	25,900	26,100	26,100	26,300	26,500	25,800	24,600	23,800	23,600
	State CAFR	16,721	16,951	17,025	16,848	16,959	17,272	16,557	15,571	15,430
	Diff	9,179	9,149	9,075	9,452	9,541	8,528	8,043	8,229	8,170
	Percent Diff	54.9%	54.0%	53.3%	56.1%	56.3%	49.4%	48.6%	52.8%	52.9%
Arizona (AZ)	U.S. BLS	81,800	82,500	83,200	83,300	84,500	86,000	86,200	87,000	89,200
	State CAFR	49,127	48,698	49,847	49,278	48,910	50,481	50,816	51,898	52,705
	Diff	32,673	33,802	33,353	34,022	35,590	35,519	35,384	35,102	36,495
	Percent Diff	66.5%	69.4%	66.9%	66.9%	72.8%	70.4%	69.6%	67.6%	69.2%
Arkansas (AR)	U.S. BLS	75,100	75,500	76,200	76,500	77,000	77,600	77,900	77,800	77,900
	State CAFR	57,109	56,751	56,705	57,421	56,944	56,956	60,816	60,520	61,559
	Diff	17,991	18,749	19,495	19,079	20,056	20,644	17,084	17,280	16,341
	Percent Diff	31.5%	33.0%	34.4%	33.2%	35.2%	36.2%	28.1%	28.6%	26.5%
California (CA)	U.S. BLS	483,500	485,400	482,200	484,300	496,700	509,400	519,700	528,000	534,000
	State CAFR	345,777	371,960	356,808	346,319	353,896	360,859	350,680	361,743	368,520
	Diff	137,723	113,440	125,392	137,981	142,804	148,541	169,020	166,257	165,480
	Percent Diff	39.8%	30.5%	35.1%	39.8%	40.4%	41.2%	48.2%	46.0%	44.9%
Colorado (CO)	U.S. BLS	93,000	95,400	97,600	107,800	109,600	112,800	116,500	121,200	125,900
	State CAFR	65,325	66,691	67,871	68,898	70,823	72,369	72,483	74,252	76,578
	Diff	27,675	28,709	29,729	38,902	38,777	40,431	44,017	46,948	49,322
	Percent Diff	42.4%	43.0%	43.8%	56.5%	54.8%	55.9%	60.7%	63.2%	64.4%
Connecticut (CT)	U.S. BLS	74,100	73,900	73,900	73,900	74,000	74,100	71,800	70,700	70,400
	State CAFR	56,252	56,362	57,045	54,978	55,188	55,922	53,720	49,973	47,147
	Diff	17,848	17,538	16,855	18,922	18,812	18,178	18,080	20,727	23,253
	Percent Diff	31.7%	31.1%	29.5%	34.4%	34.1%	32.5%	33.7%	41.5%	49.3%
Delaware (DE)	U.S. BLS	32,200	32,100	32,000	32,200	32,800	32,900	32,800	33,000	33,100
	State CAFR	32,030	32,318	32,655	32,875	33,034	32,865	32,854	33,127	33,088
	Diff	170	(218)	(655)	(675)	(234)	35	(54)	(127)	12
	Percent Diff	0.5%	(0.7%)	(2.0%)	(2.1%)	(0.7%)	0.1%	(0.2%)	(0.4%)	0.0%
District of Columbia (DC)	U.S. BLS	36,800	35,400	35,200	36,000	38,600	40,200	40,400	41,100	42,200
	State CAFR	25,857	27,235	27,209	27,402	27,560	28,826	28,983	29,863	30,829
	Diff	10,943	8,165	7,991	8,598	11,040	11,374	11,417	11,237	11,371
	Percent Diff	42.3%	30.0%	29.4%	31.4%	40.1%	39.5%	39.4%	37.6%	36.9%
Florida (FL)	U.S. BLS	248,200	250,800	245,800	245,400	246,800	249,000	251,600	255,200	257,700
	State CAFR	116,433	112,153	111,908	107,543	105,515	105,536	104,368	104,506	105,205
	Diff	131,767	138,647	133,892	137,857	141,285	143,464	147,232	150,694	152,495
	Percent Diff	113.2%	123.6%	119.6%	128.2%	133.9%	135.9%	141.1%	144.2%	145.0%
Georgia (GA)	U.S. BLS	175,500	174,800	173,800	171,400	170,300	168,800	166,300	168,400	171,100
	State CAFR	174,739	144,361	142,948	135,973	138,287	146,362	149,023	150,997	152,043
	Diff	761	30,439	30,852	35,427	32,013	22,438	17,277	17,403	19,057
	Percent Diff	0.4%	21.1%	21.6%	26.1%	23.1%	15.3%	11.6%	11.5%	12.5%
Hawaii (HI)	U.S. BLS	71,700	71,100	72,100	71,900	74,200	74,500	73,900	73,200	73,000
	State CAFR	51,398	51,033	51,247	51,574	52,017	51,609	51,538	49,680	50,461
	Diff	20,302	20,067	20,853	20,326	22,183	22,891	22,362	23,520	22,539
	Percent Diff	39.5%	39.3%	40.7%	39.4%	42.6%	44.4%	43.4%	47.3%	44.7%
Idaho (ID)	U.S. BLS	28,500	28,600	28,700	28,900	29,000	29,500	29,800	30,200	30,500
	State CAFR	23,546	23,065	23,186	23,447	23,723	23,821	24,180	25,307	24,512
	Diff	4,954	5,535	5,514	5,453	5,277	5,679	5,620	4,893	5,988
	Percent Diff	21.0%	24.0%	23.8%	23.3%	22.2%	23.8%	23.2%	19.3%	24.4%
Illinois (IL)	U.S. BLS	148,900	150,800	149,200	148,300	150,300	149,500	145,400	144,200	146,600
	State CAFR	67,742	68,146	64,328	62,836	64,055	64,470	62,719	62,081	63,027
	Diff	81,158	82,654	84,872	85,464	86,245	85,030	82,681	82,119	83,573
	Percent Diff	119.8%	121.3%	131.9%	136.0%	134.6%	131.9%	131.8%	132.3%	132.6%

State	Data	2010	2011	2012	2013	2014	2015	2016	2017	2018
Indiana (IN)	U.S. BLS	114,000	114,400	115,500	115,900	115,600	117,900	117,500	119,600	119,900
	State CAFR	34,934	34,720	33,829	33,344	33,586	33,103	33,403	33,365	33,696
	Diff	79,066	79,680	81,671	82,556	82,014	84,797	84,097	86,235	86,204
	Percent Diff	226.3%	229.5%	241.4%	247.6%	244.2%	256.2%	251.8%	258.5%	255.8%
Iowa (IA)	U.S. BLS	64,900	65,400	65,700	66,200	66,700	67,200	68,000	68,600	67,800
	State CAFR	64,110	62,103	61,831	61,168	63,838	63,916	64,490	65,017	64,904
	Diff	790	3,297	3,869	5,032	2,862	3,284	3,510	3,583	2,896
	Percent Diff	1.2%	5.3%	6.3%	8.2%	4.5%	5.1%	5.4%	5.5%	4.5%
Kansas (KS)	U.S. BLS	53,100	52,900	52,100	51,500	51,300	51,400	51,900	52,000	52,500
	State CAFR	43,090	42,735	41,201	40,361	40,127	39,772	40,102	39,943	37,173
	Diff	10,010	10,165	10,899	11,139	11,173	11,628	11,798	12,057	15,327
	Percent Diff	23.2%	23.8%	26.5%	27.6%	27.8%	29.2%	29.4%	30.2%	41.2%
Kentucky (KY)	U.S. BLS	91,100	93,700	97,900	100,800	102,200	99,400	96,900	96,200	94,300
	State CAFR	39,318	37,920	37,832	38,340	37,383	36,929	36,173	36,464	36,666
	Diff	51,782	55,780	60,068	62,460	64,817	62,471	60,727	59,736	57,634
	Percent Diff	131.7%	147.1%	158.8%	162.9%	173.4%	169.2%	167.9%	163.8%	157.2%
Louisiana (LA)	U.S. BLS	110,900	107,000	103,200	96,100	89,400	87,400	87,000	88,300	89,300
	State CAFR	95,100	88,874	85,863	75,326	70,027	69,150	68,959	70,953	69,717
	Diff	15,800	18,126	17,337	20,774	19,373	18,250	18,041	17,347	19,583
	Percent Diff	16.6%	20.4%	20.2%	27.6%	27.7%	26.4%	26.2%	24.4%	28.1%
Maine (ME)	U.S. BLS	27,500	27,100	26,900	26,700	26,600	26,100	25,800	25,700	25,500
	State CAFR	13,836	13,737	13,355	13,324	13,264	13,305	13,271	13,275	12,984
	Diff	13,664	13,363	13,545	13,376	13,336	12,795	12,529	12,425	12,516
	Percent Diff	98.8%	97.3%	101.4%	100.4%	100.5%	96.2%	94.4%	93.6%	96.4%
Maryland (MD)	U.S. BLS	113,500	112,900	110,600	111,000	110,600	110,500	108,900	109,300	110,100
	State CAFR	100,298	98,701	99,084	100,973	106,784	103,304	110,791	105,809	104,966
	Diff	13,202	14,199	11,516	10,027	3,816	7,196	(1,891)	3,491	5,134
	Percent Diff	13.2%	14.4%	11.6%	9.9%	3.6%	7.0%	(1.7%)	3.3%	4.9%
Massachusetts (MA)	U.S. BLS	123,500	123,400	124,600	128,200	133,500	132,300	131,000	129,500	129,400
	State CAFR	84,846	84,071	84,462	87,205	86,488	87,760	86,213	85,360	85,376
	Diff	38,654	39,329	40,138	40,995	47,012	44,540	44,787	44,140	44,024
	Percent Diff	45.6%	46.8%	47.5%	47.0%	54.4%	50.8%	51.9%	51.7%	51.6%
Michigan (MI)	U.S. BLS	178,600	177,500	179,700	179,100	181,000	183,700	187,600	190,500	192,200
	State CAFR	50,615	47,818	47,683	47,739	47,003	46,558	46,692	46,825	46,956
	Diff	127,985	129,682	132,017	131,361	133,997	137,142	140,908	143,675	145,244
	Percent Diff	252.9%	271.2%	276.9%	275.2%	285.1%	294.6%	301.8%	306.8%	309.3%
Minnesota (MN)	U.S. BLS	99,900	98,700	99,300	100,900	102,100	99,800	97,900	99,200	100,100
	State CAFR	51,400	51,300	49,526	51,300	51,960	51,913	51,707	52,456	53,016
	Diff	48,500	47,400	49,774	49,600	50,140	47,887	46,193	46,744	47,084
	Percent Diff	94.4%	92.4%	100.5%	96.7%	96.5%	92.2%	89.3%	89.1%	88.8%
Mississippi (MS)	U.S. BLS	61,600	60,600	60,600	60,800	61,500	60,900	60,900	60,100	59,400
	State CAFR	33,205	32,322	32,307	32,270	31,692	30,947	30,214	28,848	27,610
	Diff	28,395	28,278	28,293	28,530	29,808	29,953	30,686	31,252	31,790
	Percent Diff	85.5%	87.5%	87.6%	88.4%	94.1%	96.8%	101.6%	108.3%	115.1%
Missouri (MO)	U.S. BLS	105,200	101,300	101,000	100,700	99,500	102,000	102,100	102,700	102,900
	State CAFR	61,580	58,959	57,955	57,378	57,254	56,727	56,199	56,045	55,626
	Diff	43,620	42,341	43,045	43,322	42,246	45,273	45,901	46,655	47,274
	Percent Diff	70.8%	71.8%	74.3%	75.5%	73.8%	79.8%	81.7%	83.2%	85.0%
Montana (MT)	U.S. BLS	26,600	26,800	27,000	27,900	28,500	28,600	28,400	28,200	27,600
	State CAFR	21,698	21,997	21,968	22,547	22,761	22,991	22,892	23,061	22,849
	Diff	4,902	4,803	5,032	5,353	5,739	5,609	5,508	5,139	4,751
	Percent Diff	22.6%	21.8%	22.9%	23.7%	25.2%	24.4%	24.1%	22.3%	20.8%
Nebraska (NE)	U.S. BLS	41,000	40,700	41,100	41,400	41,500	42,200	43,400	43,200	43,400
	State CAFR*	16,016	15,839	15,902	16,283	16,379	16,445	16,160	15,910	15,858
	Diff	24,984	24,861	25,198	25,117	25,121	25,755	27,240	27,290	27,542
	Percent Diff	156.0%	157.0%	158.5%	154.3%	153.4%	156.6%	168.6%	171.5%	173.7%
Nevada (NV)	U.S. BLS	37,100	36,400	36,300	37,300	37,800	38,800	39,500	40,900	40,800
	State CAFR	26,442	25,814	25,372	25,184	26,303	26,820	27,716	29,430	30,360
	Diff	10,658	10,586	10,928	12,116	11,497	11,980	11,784	11,470	10,440
	Percent Diff	40.3%	41.0%	43.1%	48.1%	43.7%	44.7%	42.5%	39.0%	34.4%
New Hampshire (NH)	U.S. BLS	25,200	25,000	24,600	24,000	24,500	24,600	24,800	24,600	24,400
	State CAFR	18,487	17,820	17,867	17,921	17,754	17,756	17,071	16,970	17,050
	Diff	6,713	7,180	6,733	6,079	6,746	6,844	7,729	7,630	7,350
	Percent Diff	36.3%	40.3%	37.7%	33.9%	38.0%	38.5%	45.3%	45.0%	43.1%

State	Data	2010	2011	2012	2013	2014	2015	2016	2017	2018
New Jersey (NJ)	U.S. BLS	152,700	148,100	146,000	147,800	145,900	141,100	140,600	140,700	140,300
	State CAFR	74,536	72,228	69,901	69,195	68,318	66,018	64,433	64,379	64,552
	Diff	78,164	75,872	76,099	78,605	77,582	75,082	76,167	76,321	75,748
	Percent Diff	104.9%	105.0%	108.9%	113.6%	113.6%	113.7%	118.2%	118.5%	117.3%
New Mexico (NM)	U.S. BLS	59,300	57,300	56,300	57,100	58,200	56,800	56,400	55,700	55,700
	State CAFR	27,120	26,116	25,889	25,592	25,496	25,496	25,808	25,863	25,364
	Diff	32,180	31,184	30,411	31,508	32,704	31,304	30,592	29,837	30,336
	Percent Diff	118.7%	119.4%	117.5%	123.1%	128.3%	122.8%	118.5%	115.4%	119.6%
New York (NY)	U.S. BLS	260,900	259,300	254,800	252,600	251,200	250,700	254,100	257,100	256,100
	State CAFR*	260,800	259,100	254,600	252,900	250,800	250,100	253,100	257,100	256,100
	Diff	100	200	200	(300)	400	600	1,000	0	0
	Percent Diff	0.0%	0.1%	0.1%	(0.1%)	0.2%	0.2%	0.4%	0.0%	0.0%
North Carolina (NC)	U.S. BLS	204,300	203,900	202,800	204,500	202,800	201,400	201,800	202,100	203,800
	State CAFR	316,959	322,564	322,391	324,805	316,265	311,438	312,947	312,848	310,916
	Diff	(112,659)	(118,664)	(119,591)	(120,305)	(113,465)	(110,038)	(111,147)	(110,748)	(107,116)
	Percent Diff	(35.5%)	(36.8%)	(37.1%)	(37.0%)	(35.9%)	(35.3%)	(35.5%)	(35.4%)	(34.5%)
North Dakota (ND)	U.S. BLS	24,600	24,700	24,700	24,800	23,900	23,900	24,200	23,500	23,000
	State CAFR	15,685	16,052	16,062	16,177	16,368	16,639	16,598	16,118	15,675
	Diff	8,915	8,648	8,638	8,623	7,532	7,261	7,602	7,382	7,325
	Percent Diff	56.8%	53.9%	53.8%	53.3%	46.0%	43.6%	45.8%	45.8%	46.7%
Ohio (OH)	U.S. BLS	167,100	169,200	173,500	172,300	175,400	178,100	179,700	179,900	178,800
	State CAFR	54,105	52,599	50,013	48,880	48,635	48,400	48,557	48,769	48,196
	Diff	112,995	116,601	123,487	123,420	126,765	129,700	131,143	131,131	130,604
	Percent Diff	208.8%	221.7%	246.9%	252.5%	260.6%	268.0%	270.1%	268.9%	271.0%
Oklahoma (OK)	U.S. BLS	83,800	84,800	86,400	86,300	85,800	85,600	84,900	83,300	81,500
	State CAFR	35,960	34,379	33,595	34,127	34,542	34,436	33,820	32,874	31,715
	Diff	47,840	50,421	52,805	52,173	51,258	51,164	51,080	50,426	49,785
	Percent Diff	133.0%	146.7%	157.2%	152.9%	148.4%	148.6%	151.0%	153.4%	157.0%
Oregon (OR)	U.S. BLS	79,800	80,600	80,100	81,100	71,100	58,100	55,900	56,400	39,500
	State CAFR	51,106	51,106	51,227	50,614	37,919	37,929	38,753	38,752	39,803
	Diff	28,694	29,494	28,873	30,486	33,181	20,171	17,147	17,648	(303)
	Percent Diff	56.1%	57.7%	56.4%	60.2%	87.5%	53.2%	44.2%	45.5%	(0.8%)
Pennsylvania (PA)	U.S. BLS	162,500	160,200	158,500	157,500	156,900	156,500	156,500	155,700	154,800
	State CAFR	91,840	88,621	88,903	86,931	86,700	86,477	86,444	85,758	84,786
	Diff	70,660	71,579	69,597	70,569	70,200	70,023	70,056	69,942	70,014
	Percent Diff	76.9%	80.8%	78.3%	81.2%	81.0%	81.0%	81.0%	81.6%	82.6%
Rhode Island (RI)	U.S. BLS	19,500	19,600	19,700	19,900	19,900	19,700	19,900	20,000	20,000
	State CAFR	10,329	10,518	10,495	10,759	10,828	10,620	10,526	10,676	10,533
	Diff	9,171	9,082	9,205	9,141	9,072	9,080	9,374	9,324	9,467
	Percent Diff	88.8%	86.3%	87.7%	85.0%	83.8%	85.5%	89.1%	87.3%	89.9%
South Carolina (SC)	U.S. BLS	104,700	103,200	104,300	103,300	105,000	105,700	106,200	107,100	107,600
	State CAFR	68,803	66,590	66,672	36,583	36,850	37,029	37,027	37,341	37,963
	Diff	35,897	36,610	37,628	66,717	68,150	68,671	69,173	69,759	69,637
	Percent Diff	52.2%	55.0%	56.4%	182.4%	184.9%	185.5%	186.8%	186.8%	183.4%
South Dakota (SD)	U.S. BLS	18,300	18,300	18,400	18,400	18,600	18,500	18,400	18,400	18,500
	State CAFR	8,609	8,525	8,305	8,411	8,440	8,476	8,387	8,391	8,361
	Diff	9,691	9,775	10,095	10,089	10,160	10,024	10,013	10,009	10,139
	Percent Diff	112.6%	114.7%	121.6%	120.0%	120.4%	118.3%	119.4%	119.3%	121.3%
Tennessee (TN)	U.S. BLS	98,400	96,300	94,800	94,500	96,500	96,500	96,500	98,000	99,000
	State CAFR	44,612	42,609	41,908	41,785	41,023	39,968	39,288	40,302	40,600
	Diff	53,788	53,691	52,892	52,715	55,477	56,532	57,212	57,698	58,400
	Percent Diff	120.6%	126.0%	126.2%	126.2%	135.2%	141.4%	145.6%	143.2%	143.8%
Texas (TX)	U.S. BLS	408,900	399,400	394,700	396,300	396,600	397,000	404,900	409,800	412,800
	State CAFR	311,229	311,511	309,706	308,835	310,959	315,963	323,419	327,015	324,370
	Diff	97,671	87,889	84,994	87,465	85,641	81,037	81,481	82,785	88,430
	Percent Diff	31.4%	28.2%	27.4%	28.3%	27.5%	25.6%	25.2%	25.3%	27.3%
Utah (UT)	U.S. BLS	64,500	65,600	68,300	70,900	74,100	76,200	78,700	81,100	83,000
	State CAFR	20,418	20,057	19,870	20,019	19,950	19,957	20,150	20,375	20,556
	Diff	44,082	45,543	48,430	50,881	54,150	56,243	58,550	60,725	62,444
	Percent Diff	215.9%	227.1%	243.7%	254.2%	271.4%	281.8%	290.6%	298.0%	303.8%
Vermont (VT)	U.S. BLS	17,800	18,200	18,400	18,600	19,000	19,000	19,000	19,200	19,000
	State CAFR	7,651	7,669	7,743	8,011	8,127	8,218	8,182	8,377	8,350
	Diff	10,149	10,531	10,657	10,589	10,873	10,782	10,818	10,823	10,650
	Percent Diff	132.6%	137.3%	137.6%	132.2%	133.8%	131.2%	132.2%	129.2%	127.5%

State	Data	2010	2011	2012	2013	2014	2015	2016	2017	2018
Virginia (VA)	U.S. BLS	153,300	156,700	158,900	159,200	161,100	160,500	160,000	159,400	160,100
	State CAFR	110,235	111,986	117,066	117,405	117,332	117,118	125,196	125,650	123,957
	Diff	43,065	44,714	41,834	41,795	43,768	43,382	34,804	33,750	36,143
	Percent Diff	39.1%	39.9%	35.7%	35.6%	37.3%	37.0%	27.8%	26.9%	29.2%
Washington (WA)	U.S. BLS	151,400	148,400	148,100	150,200	152,900	155,900	159,800	161,100	155,600
	State CAFR	40,391	38,640	36,940	37,429	37,250	38,067	39,019	39,871	40,147
	Diff	111,009	109,760	111,160	112,771	115,650	117,833	120,781	121,229	115,453
	Percent Diff	274.8%	284.1%	300.9%	301.3%	310.5%	309.5%	309.5%	304.1%	287.6%
West Virginia (WV)	U.S. BLS	49,400	49,800	50,500	50,200	49,900	49,300	49,600	48,700	48,000
	State CAFR	35,513	36,530	37,021	37,277	36,866	36,307	35,279	34,509	34,325
	Diff	13,887	13,270	13,479	12,923	13,034	12,993	14,321	14,191	13,675
	Percent Diff	39.1%	36.3%	36.4%	34.7%	35.4%	35.8%	40.6%	41.1%	39.8%
Wisconsin (WI)	U.S. BLS	99,200	96,500	95,000	96,100	98,000	96,900	95,600	95,100	93,900
	State CAFR	64,679	64,168	64,319	65,254	66,359	66,367	64,666	65,111	65,033
	Diff	34,521	32,332	30,681	30,846	31,641	30,533	30,934	29,989	28,867
	Percent Diff	53.4%	50.4%	47.7%	47.3%	47.7%	46.0%	47.8%	46.1%	44.4%
Wyoming (WY)	U.S. BLS	15,600	15,700	15,800	15,700	15,500	15,600	15,400	15,200	14,900
	State CAFR	10,412	10,178	9,438	9,327	9,853	9,845	9,581	9,802	9,132
	Diff	5,188	5,522	6,362	6,373	5,647	5,755	5,819	5,398	5,768
	Percent Diff	49.8%	54.3%	67.4%	68.3%	57.3%	58.5%	60.7%	55.1%	63.2%

Note: Negative values are enclosed in parentheses ( ).
* The state's 2020 Corporate Annual Financial Report (CAFR) was used in lieu of the 2019 report.

APPENDIX E:
INDIVIDUAL STATE COMPREHENSIVE ANNUAL FINANCIAL REPORT (CAFR) SOURCE DATA REFERENCE

STATE	CAFR FY	CAFR PAGE	STATE	CAFR FY	CAFR PAGE
Alabama	2019	337	Kentucky	2019	278
Alaska	2019	309	Louisiana	2019	204
Arizona	2019	294	Maine	2019	254
Arkansas	2019	200	Maryland	2019	156
California	2019	328	Massachusetts	2019	212
Colorado	2019	280	Michigan	2019	308
Connecticut	2019	204	Minnesota	2019	292
Delaware	2019	178	Mississippi	2019	162
District of Columbia	2019	217	Missouri	2019	235
Florida	2019	310	Montana	2019	319
Georgia	2019	372	Nebraska	2020	175
Hawaii	2019	173	Nevada	2019	185
Idaho	2019	191	New Hampshire	2019	158
Illinois	2019	378	New Jersey	2019	388
Indiana	2019	267	New Mexico	2019	352
Iowa	2019	226	New York	2020	246
Kansas	2019	169	North Carolina	2019	352

STATE	CAFR FY	CAFR PAGE
North Dakota	2019	232
Ohio	2019	314
Oklahoma	2019	222
Oregon	2019	273
Pennsylvania	2019	287
Rhode Island	2019	290
South Carolina	2019	296
South Dakota	2019	189
Tennessee	2019	236

STATE	CAFR FY	CAFR PAGE
Texas	2019	331
Utah	2019	236
Vermont	2019	275
Virginia	2019	348
Washington	2019	315
West Virginia	2019	306
Wisconsin	2019	250
Wyoming	2019	240

APPENDIX F:
ARITHMETIC REFRESHER

Average and Median

Set A and Set B in the table below have the same average value. But the median values, that is the middle value of the sorted list of values, are different.

Value #	1	2	3	4	5	6	7	8	9	Average	Median
Set A	90	80	70	60	50	40	30	20	10	50.0	50
Set B	442	1	1	1	1	1	1	1	1	50.0	1

Summation Series

Given a set of n values: $x_1 , x_2 , x_3 , x_4 , x_5 , \ldots , x_n$

$$\sum_{i=1}^{n} x_i = x_1 + x_2 + x_3 + x_4 + x_5 + \ldots + x_n$$

Alphabetical Index

Allopoly..
   allopolistic loss...
      definition...25
      measurement...59
   allopoly prevention..35
   allopoly progression..36
   allopoly succession..37
   allopoly vs culture..49
   analytical implications..66
   anonymity...31
   benefits...25
   collusion...27
   communication..28
   comparative advantage..26
   cooperation, secrecy, coercion and force.................................26
   corporation..47
   corruption..68
   debt...39
   definition..17
   demand elasticity...
      high..51
      low..51, 78, 121
   diffuse acquisition and concentrated collection...............33, 113
   dishonesty...27
   disparity in secrecy, coercion and force....................................29
   driving force of allopoly creation...19
   economic principles..18
   education...31
   government allopolies...67
   greed..19
   imputed morality..41
   law..51
   local non-satiation..19
   multiplicative and cascade effect of allopolistic loss.................
      due to corruption...130
      due to dishonesty...42
      due to imposed allopolistic loss..51
      through a supply chain...25
   non-government allopolies...67
   objective of an allopoly...59
   preference to form allopolies with governing allopolies.............24

private enterprise...11
professions..40
profit...11
quality of life...32
resources with inelastic demand......................................127
rule and law violations and changes.................................42
simultaneous operation of multiple effects.....................28
standards...39
structure..21
technology...45
    shift from radical to incremental advances..................46
    technological advancement offsets..............................46
time as an economic measure...57
traditional economic analyses..18
travel...30
usury..39
values..41
    value shift from long to short term...............................42
veblen goods..66
Cycle Of Civilization..
    arc of a culture's technological advancement................65
    continuity of a level of technology...............................64
    cycle of civilization (with time as a metric)...................77
    decline of..78, 80
    driving force behind the cycle of civilization................53
    education and time...63
    historical time cost..60
    measurement basis for social and technological development....60
    number of educated individuals....................................64
    rate of a civilization's technological development........63
    riddle of allopoly formation and civilization................55
    rise of...77, 79
    time vs. currency..79
Government...
    concealment...74
    corruption..69
        laundering of illegally obtained evidence................75
    definition...15
    draining the swamp...71
    functional requirements..23
    imputed morality...24
    interest payments..101
    is a government too intrusive?....................................128

lawsuit award caps..69
medicine...121
oversight..70
patronage...72
pensions...121
private enterprise..11
transfer payments...102
Slavery...
  a type of allopoly...83
  allopolistic characteristics of slavery...81
  analytical discontinuity..16
  categories of...83
    manipulation of law and economic conditions to create an
    oversupply of workers..85
    the enslaved are property...84
  consent...85, 90, 118
  definition...16, 55, 86
  interpretation of the slavery tax rate...90
    specific interpretation...118
  isolation from society..84
  supported by the government...83
Slavery Tax Rate...83
  business...104
  children...113
  difference from a flat tax...110
  elderly...116
  fairness...99
  government interest payments..101
  government transfer payments..102
  government workers...92
    government worker costs...94
    slavery tax rate due to government workers.................................92
  higher level government's usurpation of power from lower
  government levels through the use of taxes..................................102
  implementation..104, 109
  incarcerated...121
  indigent...120
  infirm..120
  interpretation of the slavery tax rate...90
    for business..104
    government workers..90
    specific interpretation...118
    time-based metric..99

non-labor costs and specific amounts................................96
objective target for tax reduction................................125
other government wards...121
population.. 94
regressive taxes..103
retirees..113
slavery tax rate using real data..................................105
spouses and significant others....................................113
unemployment..114

Index of Theorems

THEOREM #1:   The Driving Force of Allopoly Creation...............19

THEOREM #2:   Allopoly Structure..................................22

THEOREM #3:   Preference to Form Allopolies with Governing
                Allopolies..24

THEOREM #4:   Increasing Disparity in Secrecy, Coercion and Force
               29

THEOREM #5:   The Driving Force Behind the Cycle of Civilization
               53

THEOREM #6:   The Riddle of Allopoly Formation and Civilization
               55

THEOREM #7:   Time as an Economic Measure.........................57

THEOREM #8:   Goods and Services are Accumulations of Time.
                Absent Fluctuations in its Value so is Money.......58

THEOREM #9:   The Objective of an Allopoly........................59

THEOREM #10:   Measurement of Allopolistic Loss...................59

THEOREM #11:   Measurement Basis for Social and Technological
                Development..60

THEOREM #12:   Rate of a Civilization's Technological Development
               63

THEOREM #13:   Education and Time.................................63

THEOREM #14:   The Slavery Tax Rate due to Government Workers.
               92

Index of Corollaries

COROLLARY #1:   Allopoly Secrecy, Cooperation, Coercion, and Force...26

COROLLARY #2:   Reduction of Target Allopoly Secrecy...............30

COROLLARY #3:   Increasing Control of Communication..............30

COROLLARY #4:   Reduction of Anonymity.....................................31

COROLLARY #5:   Reduction of Education Level............................32

COROLLARY #6:   Increasing Disparity in the Quality of Life.........33

COROLLARY #7:   Value Shift from Long to Short Term................42

COROLLARY #8:   Multiplicative and Cascade Effect of Allopolistic Loss..51

COROLLARY #9:   Technological Advancement Versus the Number of Educated Individuals.....................................64

COROLLARY #10: Continuity of a Level of Technology..................64

COROLLARY #11: The Arc of a Culture's Technological Advancement...65

COROLLARY #12: Game Theory...67

COROLLARY #13: Reduction of Target Allopoly Mobility...............81

Index of Questions

QUESTION #1:   How does the Slavery Tax Rate differ from a flat tax?..110

QUESTION #2:   Should all taxes be counted against the slavery tax rate?..111

QUESTION #3:   Should government-mandated purchases of products or services from either government or non-government entities be counted as a tax?...112

QUESTION #4:   Should only full-time government workers be counted in (G)?..112

QUESTION #5:   Should all the population be counted in (P)?.......112

QUESTION #6:   How does the Slavery Tax Rate apply to those unable to work who receive government benefits? 116

QUESTION #7:   How many government workers are required for each citizen?...122

QUESTION #8:   Is a government spending too much?.................125

QUESTION #9:   What is the appropriate level of technology a government should provide in the way of government provided technological infrastructure? 125

QUESTION #10:   Is a student receiving a government-subsidized education a government employee?...................126

QUESTION #11:   How is non-tax imposed allopolistic loss tallied? 127

QUESTION #12:   Is a government too intrusive?...........................128

WHAT IS NEXT?

The number of U.S. state and sub-state government hierarchies (38,829 in 2017) make the collection of data from state, county and municipal governments a daunting task.

Volunteers are needed to obtain government employment and non-labor expense data from the state, county and municipal governments in which they reside.

This work can be made part of an individual or collaborative educational research project that is easily graded by the instructor in the form of a checklist.

To volunteer please send an email stating the United States government hierarchies in which you reside (state, county and municipality) to <u>volunteer@slaverytaxrate.ch</u> .

When sufficient interest exists, you may be contacted.

Cover Graphics

The Tomb of Menna. (circa 1490 BC) Ancient Egyptian tomb painting. Retrieved from https://historyview.org/library/tomb-of-menna/ .

Ancient Roman stone relief. (circa 0-200 AD?). Retrieved from http://www.historyshistories.com/roman-republic-activity.html .

Meister der Apokalypsenrose der Sainte Chapelle (circa 1480-1510 AD) *Le Livre de richesse: seigneur percevant l'impôt, extrait des Traités théologique.* Retrieved from https://commons.wikimedia.org/wiki/File:Tax_payment_to_a_lord_-_BNF_Fr9608_f11v.jpg .